Paul Rogers has been my go-to 'mentor' o
I first got involved in green politics in the
brings all his unique expertise, wisdom
unprecedentedly disrupted world. And what an exiιαυιω.....,
library' he and Judith Large have created in the process.
Jonathan Porritt, Sustainability Campaigner and Author

In a world of interlocked crises, there is an urgent need to counteract hope-
lessness and wilful ignorance. This short book, written by two authorities
in peace studies and well-experienced practitioners, offers an informed
and persuasive account of key interconnected and current security threats.
It stresses the importance of human security, and advocates for a less de-
fensive and militaristic approach to protecting our future. The authors
suggest actions at individual, community and societal levels which in time
may help to divert us from the (in)security trap and inhumanity linked to
exclusivist politics and economics profiting from it. The book also provides
useful resources for information, mobilization and solidarity for those who
may be inspired to know and do more.
Associate Professor Catalina Montoya, Director of the Archbishop
Desmond Tutu Centre for War and Peace Studies, Liverpool Hope
University

Few if any prophets have been so calm, steady and thoroughly vindicated
as Paul Rogers. At the time he warned that if the USA invaded Iraq it
would initiate a disastrous thirty year war that would spread out across
the Middle East and suck America to defeat. And here we are, only two-
thirds of the way through. Equally, he emphasised at the start of the cen-
tury the twin dangers of climate change and hi-tech bellicosity. Free from
florid rhetoric, incredibly patient and rooted in careful research, he needs
to be read and listened to. Now in this lucid overview of the current 'poly-
crisis' he sets out what can be done before it is too late.
Anthony Barnett, co-founder and former editor of openDemocracy

Paul Rogers has long been a source of insight, inspiration and support
to those of us reaching for a deeper analysis of global peace and security
issues. This short book offers a remarkably concise and accessible over-
view of the interlinked environmental, economic and security challenges
that shape our current trajectory, pointing us towards the work required to
build a sustainable future for people and the planet.
Celia McKeon, Chief Executive, Two Ridings Community Foundation

The Insecurity Trap

A Short Guide to Transformation

Hawthorn Press

Hawthorn Press
Published by Hawthorn Press, Hawthorn House,
1 Lansdown Lane, Stroud, Gloucestershire, GL5 1BJ, UK
Tel: (01453) 757040 E-mail: info@hawthornpress.com
Website: www.hawthornpress.com

Cover image and design © Joe Magee
Illustrations © Joe Magee
Typesetting by Lucy Guenot
Printed by Short Run Press Ltd, Exeter
Printed on environmentally friendly chlorine-free paper sourced from renewable forest stock.

Many thanks to The Sir James Reckitt Charity for their generous support of this publication.

British Library Cataloguing in Publication Data applied for

ISBN 978-1-912480-95-1
eISBN 978-1-912480-97-5

The Insecurity Trap

A Short Guide to Transformation

Paul Rogers

With Judith Large

Hawthorn Press

Dedication

For Tyoma and James

CONTENTS

Setting the Scene

There will be readers of this book who are experiencing directly how 'global security' issues affect their daily lives: higher energy prices, the disruption of supply chains, daily exposure to images and reporting from conflict zones of suffering and war, fewer and more expensive food supplies, homelessness, air pollution, floods, or disruption from climate crisis. Others know first-hand the grief and loss incurred by war, the experience of dislocation or being a target of hate because of identity affiliation and nothing more. These are the intersecting experiences of insecurity. They can be numbing, or overwhelming. To respond or act effectively, we need an understanding of what is happening and how to navigate it. We need to know our part of the whole.

The work of Paul Rogers has been dedicated to providing such a big picture. The first edition of his *Losing Control: Global Security in the Twenty-First Century* was published just before the 9/11 attacks on the Twin Towers in the US in 2001. In it he introduced the concept of 'liddism', a tendency for Western states to attempt to control threats to international security by military means, rather than by understanding their nature and the underlying factors and thus countering them at source. This approach has been compared to a pressure cooker where every attempt is made to keep the lid on, instead of turning down the heat. One of Rogers' early observations regarding global security was that well-off industrialised states were vulnerable to attack on their centres from small, disaffected non-state actors who could leverage pressure on vulnerable targets. Observing precedents in IRA (Irish Republican Army) attacks in UK urban areas, and the attempted 1993 bombing at the World Trade Center in New York, he reflected on possible US reactions in the event of a wholescale attack.

The opening of the twenty-first century came in the wake of the 1989 fall of the Berlin Wall, the collapse of the Soviet Union and a reconfiguration of the post-1945 world order. There was talk of the end of history, the triumph of democracy (or, some said, capitalism) and a new international system. But in that last decade of the twentieth century former Soviet states imploded with violent civil wars and re-emergent 'frozen conflicts' along ethnic and territorial lines (Abkhazia, Nagorno-Karabakh, South Ossetia, Transnistria). In 1994, during a period of about a hundred days, some 500,000 to 800,000 people were killed in the Rwanda genocide. Bitter war raged during the dissolution and wars of Yugoslavia from 1991 to 1995 and again in 1999 over Kosovo.

And yet UN Secretary-General Boutros Boutros-Ghali's 1992 'Agenda for Peace' was a foundational statement of the UN's role in stabilising the post-Cold-War world.[1] It welcomed the end of Cold War 'distrust and hostility' between superpowers and detailed how the UN – assisted by a functioning Security Council – could operationalise work on preventive diplomacy, peacekeeping, peacemaking and post-conflict peacebuilding. This blueprint for a proactive, interventionist UN set the terms for policy discussions about the legitimacy of intervention for the ensuing three decades. It set the stage for new cooperation and the multilateral demonstration of a rules-based order.

For an international rules-based system (as enshrined in the founding of the United Nations) to be effective, the rules must be seen to be observed by their principal and most powerful advocates. It follows that the post-9/11 decision by the George W. Bush administration to invade Iraq in 2003 (under a contested UN authorisation) cast a long shadow over the US claim to be the champion and defender of a rules-based international system. The subsequent failure to close the Guantanamo Bay detention facility, the use of torture in US operations, and the continued use of presidential 'War on Terror' directives to carry out lethal drone strikes in

---

1. See Boutros Boutros-Ghali, *An Agenda for Peace: Preventive Diplomacy, Peacemaking and Peace-Keeping*, New York, UN, 1992, https://digitallibrary.un.org/record/145749?ln=en

the Middle East and Pakistan (often with ensuing civilian deaths)[2] have left the United States open to accusations that it is selective about when it does and does not abide by the international norms and rules that it expects others to comply with. Some critics say this has opened space for other countries to pursue a 'might is right' approach in their own policies. International capacity to deliver humanitarian assistance or to convene conflict resolution processes has suffered, or even failed, as in Afghanistan, Syria, Ukraine and Gaza. Moreover, Western emphasis on a rules-based order is coming to be seen as hypocritical and aimed only at preserving self-interest or Western domination.

The 2024 annual report from the Munich Security Conference observes that the world has entered a new era of decline in global cooperation, in favour of zero-sum thinking and advantage-seeking through protectionism, self-interest and rejection of multilateral cooperation.[3] It identifies a trend towards transactional thinking that favours short-term goals. This is in a time of need for the entire planet, when climate change has no respect for borders or national interest, and human beings are experiencing their interdependence every day.

Four editions of *Losing Control* have now addressed such issues. This summary volume exists in a context that has changed from the circumstances in which *Losing Control* was first published over two decades ago. Along with the decline of multilateralism and UN legitimacy, there are other factors to bear in mind when reading *The Insecurity Trap*:

1. *Shifts in governance and response to democracy projects.* Electoral democracy is functioning, even flourishing. In 2024 more citizens than ever in history will cast their votes in at least 64 countries (as well as the European Union) –

---

2. See proceedings of Chatham House / London Conference 2015, https://www.chathamhouse.org/sites/default/files/London%20Conference%202015%20-%20Background%20Papers.pdf

3. See 'Lose–Lose?', Munich Security Report 2024, https://securityconference.org/en/publications/munich-security-report-2024/executive-summary/

representing about 49% of the people in the world – that are scheduled to hold national elections. But democracy is much more than just holding elections. For at the same time (and foreshadowed by Victor Orban's early declaration that Hungary was an 'illiberal democracy') the nature of leadership and governance has increasingly shifted to tighter, centralised, more autocratic rule and in many cases the rolling back of state provision of public services.

In a corresponding development we see what has been called 'the New Checks and Balances'[4] as citizens take initiatives and organise for reform, whether in relation to social responsibility and inclusion, climate, poverty reduction, or defence. Human rights organisations, civil society networks and non-governmental organisations, popular movements, advocacy campaigns and investigative journalists are all playing an irreplaceable role in promoting social justice and change.

2. *A rise in populism and nationalist movements.* India, long proud to be the world's largest democracy, is led by Hindu nationalist Narendra Modi; recent elections in the Netherlands, Italy and Sweden saw success for right-wing populist parties (Geert Wilders and his Freedom Party, the Brothers of Italy, Sweden Democrats). Between June 2016 and the end of 2017 there were major upheavals with the victory of Leave in Britain's European Union referendum, the election of Donald Trump as president of the United States, and unprecedented support for Marine Le Pen of the Front National in France. Jair Bolsonaro is now barred from running for office in Brazil but continues to command support in rallies and public mobilisation. Vladimir Putin's reinvention of nationalist history and subsequent military campaign has brought catastrophic war for Ukraine and untold suffering for the Russian people.

3. *Increased mistrust of institutions and science.* For many, the

---

4. International IDEA and Global State of Democracy Initiative, 'The New Checks and Balances: Global State of Democracy Report 2023', https://www.idea.int/gsod/2023/

global COVID-19 pandemic altered the relationship between citizen and state as well as causing countless personal tragedies of loss, bereavement, and disruption of income generation and daily life. The scale of social vulnerability plus the availability of social media has contributed to a rise in the denial of science and in new conspiracy theories on both the origin of the virus and the intent of governance. Conspiracy theory extends to the denial of climate change and even Holocaust denial. Based on closed thinking and 'truth', it preys on the vulnerable by offering certainty and is difficult to dispute with rational argument, because (by definition) all opposing or alternative views are part of the conspiracy. Often a viable counter-narrative is the demonstration effect of robust civic groups and the creative options they bring.

4. *The rise and speed of electronic media able to influence and control.* Social media platforms have dramatically changed communication. They set social standards, enable relationship-building, express and negotiate values, deliver news. In the process, they have also become safe enclosed spaces for the spread of hate, conspiracy theories and disinformation. By design, algorithms feed and fuel views already held, ever reinforcing beliefs, interests, or opinion trajectories. Social media hold the power to educate and inspire creativity or to instigate and incite mob violence; to inform and entertain or to bully and attack. We face regulatory challenges on discernment between free speech and hate. Facebook formally apologised for its role in Sri Lanka's 2018 anti-Muslim riots after an investigation found that incendiary content may have led to the deadly violence.[5] On the other hand, climate activists and change agents working to campaign for tax reform, reduce poverty or support refugees are building communicative communities via social media.

---

5. Tasnim Nazeer, 'Facebook's Apology for Its Role in Sri Lanka's Anti-Muslim Riots Should Spark Change', *The Diplomat*, 15 May 2020, https://thediplomat.com/2020/05/facebooks-apology-for-its-role-in-sri-lankas-anti-muslim-riots-should-spark-change/

As high-speed wireless internet becomes more available world-wide in public spaces, businesses, taxi drivers and market traders in Nairobi or Liverpool can take payment by mobile phone; Sri Lankan fishing communities receive advance tsunami alerts by phone; and photos taken via phones at scenes of violence may be circulated instantly, as for example with the death of George Floyd and in the subsequent Black Lives Matter movement. Thus, we have unprecedented sources of instant documentation for purposes of accountability and justice.

All these circumstances give us entry points as individuals or in groups or communities to work counter to the insecurity trap of climate change, economic injustice and inequality, and militarism. Let the big picture presented by Paul Rogers in this book serve as a landscape to navigate. Let it empower us to act.

Judith Large

INTRODUCTION

A Short Guide to Transformation

More than fifty years ago, the economic geographer Edwin Brooks warned of the risk of a 'crowded glowering planet of massive inequalities of wealth buttressed by stark force yet endlessly threated by desperate men in the global ghettoes'. His phrasing seemed thoroughly dystopian then but is all too believable now.[6]

In the past few years we have come through the COVID-19 pandemic that killed over twenty million people as well as increasing economic hardship and poverty, especially across the Global South. Two wars, in Ukraine and Gaza, have been added to existing conflicts in Myanmar and the Sahel region of Africa, a brutal civil war has engulfed Sudan, millions have been displaced in the long war in the Democratic Republic of the Congo and there are increasing tensions over the status of Taiwan.

The conflicts are serious enough, but they are elements in a global pattern of insecurity made worse by two other trends. One is the marginalisation of hundreds of millions, if not billions, of people across the world and not just in the Global South, and this leading to increased bitterness and anger as well as aiding the growth of extreme paramilitary movements. On top of this is the recognition, finally, that the world's climate is changing for the worst, and rapidly. The term 'existential threat' is frequently overused but global heating really is taking humanity in the direction of societal breakdown unless radical change comes, and quickly.

---

6. Edwin Brooks, 'The Implications of Ecological Limits to Development in Terms of Expectations and Aspirations in Developed and Less Developed Countries', in *Human Ecology and World Development*, edited by Anthony Vann and Paul Rogers, London, Plenum Press, 1973.

A sense of unease is increasingly expressed in social parlance that 'things are falling apart'. Prices are rising but provision of goods and services is falling. Homelessness and food banks are both on the rise. Perhaps ironically, domestic measures introduced early in the twenty-first century for the War on Terror and later for Countering Violent Extremism (CVE) did not contribute to a sense of security or cohesion, but instead added to suspicion and division among communities.

In short, it looks like a very troubled decade or more ahead, and many changes are urgently needed. This is where the 'insecurity trap' comes in. A bitterly divided world really is facing limits to growth, but this is in a pervasive culture that prioritises a security approach of hard militarism to provide Brooks's 'buttress' to protect the better off. Each challenge is seen as requiring a tough response to that challenge alone, and little thought is given to where the challenge is coming from.

If we are to respond to the underlying causes, three linked questions must be considered:

- Can we come to terms in time with the environmental limits to growth?
- Can we transform the world economy to ensure that there is far better sharing of what we have?
- Can we change our understanding and practice of international security to focus on a human security approach that works for all, not a minority elite?

Many other issues will affect our expectations and fears for the future, but these three questions are likely to be central to the world of the near future, especially the next decade. It is inevitable that people get thoroughly depressed by the state of the world, but there are powerful arguments in favour of a more positive future, especially if we recognise that we as individuals can make a difference when we work together.

The immediate task, and the reason for this short book, is to summarise current trends in the three fields of environment, economy and security; analyse how they are connected in an overarching insecurity trap; and look ahead to the positive possibilities of change, including suggestions for responses as individuals and communities.

CHAPTER ONE

Limits to Growth

Climate Breakdown

The most pressing aspect of global limits to growth is climate breakdown. The main international process for facing up to that is a UN body that meets every year, the most recent session being the 28th Session of the Conference of the Parties to the UN Framework on Climate Change. That mouthful is helpfully abbreviated to 'COP 28'.

The COPs have had a chequered history, mainly through their repeated failure to deliver agreements to limit the main cause of climate change, carbon dioxide emissions from the burning of fossil fuels. COP15 in Copenhagen back in 2009, for example, started with high hopes but finished as a damp squib with little achieved. COP21 in Paris in 2015 was more successful and set a series of clear targets. Since then, though, the achievements in subsequent COPs have not lived up to expectations, especially when measured against the accelerating changes in climate and the greatly enhanced knowledge about why they are happening. That doesn't mean that it is now too late, but it is essential to understand the reasons for the persistent lack of progress.

This is helped by putting the whole 'limits to growth' issue in a broad perspective, with an emphasis on a series of changes during the mid-1970s. This may seem an unnecessary detour, but it is not, since that decade set in motion trends that have helped determine why we are in such a mess now as well as providing a clue as to how to get out of it. A good place to start is even a bit earlier, with the achievements of two remarkable women in the 1950s and 1960s, and two stand-out books published in 1962 and 1972, *Silent Spring* and *Limits to Growth*.[7]

In the early post-war years an experienced fisheries biologist in the United States, Rachel Carson, was a gifted science writer, responsible for two bestselling books in the 1950s on marine ecology, *The Sea Around Us* (1951) and *The Edge of the Sea* (1955).[8] Her next project related to concern during the 1950s about the marked decline in bird populations, especially in farming areas that relied heavily on new types of organophosphorus pesticides. Direct links between the two were made through some nifty research by ecologists. Carson looked at this in detail and published her findings in *Silent Spring*.

This lifted the lid on the impact of the poisoning of birds as a marker of wider ecological effects. The agrochemical industry was bitterly opposed to the implications of Carson's writing. She was subject to persistent personal attacks, but was also supported by many scientists working in the field. Her book went on to have a huge transnational impact and was one of the key texts that contributed to growing awareness of the impact of human activity on the world's environments. Individual disasters such as the *Torrey Canyon* tanker wreck in 1967 contributed to this.[9] One of the worst was the terrible Aberfan tragedy of 1966 when a coal-mining waste heap collapsed and engulfed a school in the Welsh mining town of Aberfan, killing 144 people, including 116 children in the village school.[10]

By the start of the 1970s, attention across much of the Global North was focusing on environmental problems, one

---

7. Rachel Carson, *Silent Spring*, New York, Houghton Mifflin, 1962; Dennis Meadows, Donella Meadows, Jorgen Randers and William W. Behrens III, *Limits to Growth*, Switzerland, Club of Rome, 1972.

8. Rachel Carson, *The Sea Around Us*, Oxford, Oxford University Press, 1951; Rachel Carson, *The Edge of the Sea*, New York, Houghton Mifflin, 1955.

9. Tim Harford, 'Lessons from the Wreck of the Torrey Canyon', *Financial Times*, 15 February 2019.

10. Meilan Solly, 'The True Story of the Aberfan Disaster', *Smithsonian Magazine*, 15 November 2019.

response being the UN Conference on the Human Environment in Stockholm in 1972. Around that time, another book came out that went on to set the tone for much of that decade. It also countered a concern across much of the Global South that 'environmentalism' was all about the industrial Northern states cleaning up their own mess while ignoring the far greater issues of poverty and environmental exploitation in the rest of the world.

This is where *Limits to Growth* comes in. This book was the product of some early systems research by a team at Massachusetts Institute of Technology led by Donella Meadows. The research produced a predictive model of the entire global environment and the human activities within it and reached the stark conclusion that increasing human activity, if not reined in, would have a disastrous impact on the biosphere, the entire global ecosystem that contains all life. Societal collapse was likely, not in the immediate future but certainly within a few decades.

Limits to Growth was not well received in economic and political circles, the economic consensus being that technological developments would be brought in sufficiently early to cope with any problems. Any other view was utterly misplaced and thoroughly doomsday. Despite this the book had a huge impact and served the important function of giving added weight to the issues raised by the Global South at the Stockholm conference.

As if to confirm the idea of limits to growth, barely eighteen months after the Stockholm conference came the sudden massive surge in oil prices engineered by a newly powerful coalition, the Organization of the Petroleum Exporting Countries (OPEC). This process started in mid-October 1973 because Arab members of OPEC were desperate to put pressure on the US and other Western states to persuade Israel to agree to an early ceasefire in the Yom Kippur/Ramadan War. They started by announcing a 70% price rise. Not only did that stick, but it was followed by further price hikes agreed by the entire membership of OPEC.

In the 2020s we have seen plenty of fluctuations in world energy prices, most following on from oil price changes, but these have rarely been more than 10% or 20% rises. What happened from October 1973 to May 1974 was mind-boggling in comparison. During those seven months there was an overall increase in oil prices of well over 400%. To make matters worse, this coincided with a major world food crisis and a surge in other commodity prices, including metals and fertilisers.

International cooperation helped avoid a famine, but the economic impact of the energy price surge was felt throughout the decade, leading to the appearance of a rare phenomenon on the world economic scene, 'stagflation', which combined high unemployment rates with inflation. This, in turn, made it easier for the mixed model economy of the Keynesian era to be supplanted by neoliberal ideology, especially by the Reagan and Thatcher governments, whose market fundamentalism sidelined environmental concerns. As we shall see in the next chapter, this ideology put a premium on the power of the free market and had little interest in the kind of cooperative intergovernmental action needed to take on the truly global issue of climate breakdown.

The one upside of this was that the decade saw an early surge of interest in renewable energy resources, including wind turbines and solar panels, and plenty of interest in alternative low-impact lifestyles. Thirty years later, many the people who saw the sense of this very different approach back in the late 1970s and early 1980s were at the forefront of renewed concerns as the thinking behind limits to growth and the impact of climate change at last came to the fore.

Although the potential impact of carbon dioxide emissions was recognised back in the 1970s, this topic only began to have a substantive impact in political and policy circles in the early 1990s, one result being the Kyoto Protocol. This was an early intergovernmental plan to curb the burning of fossil fuels – oil, gas and coal. Signed in 1997, it set targets to comply with the 1992 United Nations Framework Convention on Climate Change. Progress was very slow even though climate modelling was pointing to enormous problems ahead. This reluctance to respond owed to both specific and more general factors.

Corporations involved in fossil fuel production and use, together with major coal-, gas- and oil-producing countries, were united in opposing governmental action to curb their activities. Even when internal assessments by the oil and gas corporations themselves supported the predictions from national and international think tanks, they would simply be ignored as the corporations spent many millions of dollars on lobbying for their activities. Such lobbying appears to have begun in the 1980s but has been a consistent feature of the anti-climate-change lobby, a very powerful system that is probably the greatest obstacle to a much needed low-carbon future.

There was also generic opposition that came from numerous neoliberal think tanks and plenty of politicians. All were strongly opposed to governmental and intergovernmental action on climate issues. In the early years there was almost complete denial of any human cause of climate change. Even when the evidence increased that the rapid burning of fossil fuels was the root cause of climate change, it was still dismissed and regarded as certainly not the responsibility of governments.

This situation was made worse by the political positions of some leading governments, especially those of major carbon emitters such as the US during the Bush and Trump administrations. Those two administrations were responsible for twelve years of backtracking and delays, but they were not alone. Australia, Russia and the Middle East oil producers were also major parts of the problem. Until the late 2010s there was little sign of change.

Despite the efforts of campaigners and climate policy specialists, only in the past five years since 2020 have climate issues really come to the fore, and radical decarbonisation has now become essential as well as hugely urgent. In 2020 the UN's Intergovernmental Panel on Climate Change (IPCC) published an assessment of what was needed to prevent catastrophic climate breakdown. This reported the radical cuts in carbon emissions needed to prevent huge problems in the coming years. To curb increases in carbon emissions and avoid a global temperature rise of over 1.5°C, a 40% decrease in global emissions would be needed by 2030. That meant a 7% decrease per year throughout the 2020s. By 2023, not only was that not being achieved, but with continuing rather than decreasing emissions we shall now have to decarbonise at a rate of over 10% a year from 2024 until the end of the decade.

On current trends that is near impossible without an immense change in attitudes and activities, and we are far more likely to go well above a 1.5°C rise. What does that mean? The many recent extreme weather disasters – in Canada, Mediterranean Europe, Hawaii, Pakistan, India and many other countries – are just a start. The world will continue to heat up; floods, droughts, heat domes, intense storms and other disasters will all increase in intensity and frequency. Many more parts of the world will experience catastrophes, costs of damage will shoot up, food shortages will get more severe, many millions of people will progressively seek to migrate, and the response will be strong political pressure in the richer states to close the castle gates and concentrate even more than at present on looking after themselves.

Most important, and invariably forgotten, is that it doesn't end there. The idea that a more carbon-dioxide-rich atmosphere will simply take us to a new warmer but stable planet that we can get used to is dangerously wrong. What will happen is that the entire system will become less and less stable for as long as the emissions continue and more heat energy is concentrated in the atmosphere. Moreover, since it takes many years for carbon dioxide to decrease naturally, even if we were now to cut emissions to zero overnight, we would still have to respond to more frequent disasters for a generation or more.

The urgency of the climate breakdown issue was potently illustrated early in January 2024 when data from the European Union's Copernicus Climate Change Service (CCCS) showed that 2023 had been, by a considerable margin, the hottest year ever recorded, 1.48°C hotter than 2022 and 0.17°C hotter than the previous record of 2016. It was dangerously close to the advisory maximum of 1.5°C higher than the world's pre-industrial average and moved the global community into uncharted territory.

That really does sound thoroughly doomwatch, but there is another, more positive side to this bleak and foreboding future, since there are three distinct reasons for optimism.

First is the change in public attitudes in many countries, especially among younger people. That has increased markedly in the past decade. Previously, it was a small minority who insisted that there had to be change, but now it is even becoming received wisdom that climate breakdown is the pre-eminent global challenge facing humankind.

Second are the impressive developments in climate science since the 1990s. New climate models combined with much more data, the use of more powerful computers, and greater numbers of scientists working in the field all mean a better understanding of how the world's climate works, which in turn increases confidence in the predictions that can be made.

Finally, there is a remarkable change in a whole range of technologies that make radical decarbonisation possible within a very few years. This means that cutting global emissions by the 40% required by 2030 could still be done – just. In many parts of the world, it is already cheaper, and often much cheaper, to generate electricity from renewable energy sources such as solar and wind than from coal, oil and gas or from nuclear reactors. Impressive developments in photovoltaic systems for using solar radiation have cut the cost of new installations by more than half, with even more improvements in the pipeline, and developments in wind turbine technology have also brought costs down. Much more needs to be done in terms of distribution and storage but the overall change is still remarkable.

That sounds good, but there is vast divide between what *could* be done and what *will* be done. The harsh fact is that the persistent downgrading of the issue by the fossil fuel industry, with its worldwide array of lobbyists, remains a huge obstacle to change despite the advantages of the lower costs of renewables. It seems incredibly short-sighted, but this global network of producer corporations and countries is determined to stretch out the profitability of fossil carbon for decades, whatever the longer-term costs to the world.

One might expect that an industry that represented a planetary threat could be subject to severe sanctions to force it to change, but fossil carbon has been the driving force of the global economy for two centuries and its resistance to change is exacerbated by that neoliberal economic model, based on an ideology of market fundamentalism. It is essential to recognise this, and where this ideology came from and why it is so deeply entrenched, both to responding to climate breakdown but also to understanding the deep economic divisions that persist across the globe.

CHAPTER TWO

It's the Economy, Stupid!

Socio-economic divisions and their impact, including the origins and impacts of neoliberalism

Neoliberal dawn

Bill Clinton, US president from 1992 to 2000, is credited with that phrase when he ran for office. By the 1990s economic neoliberalism had already been entrenched in many economies for a decade. Although neoliberal thinking had its origins in the 1930s and was in many ways reminiscent of nineteenth-century economics, it came to the fore in the three decades from 1950, following on from the work of Friedrich Hayek, Milton Friedman and others, plus the formation of the influential Mont Pelerin Society in 1947.

During the 1950s the world economic system was broadly divided into centrally planned economies such as the Soviet Union – and its satellites in Eastern Europe – China, and the market economies across most of the rest of the world. Many of the latter economies had a mixed model involving elements of social welfare, quite a high degree of government intervention, and public ownership of some industries and services.

Much of that applied only to domestic economies whereas the international political economy was largely geared to the North–South trading system of manufactured goods traded for raw materials. The origins of that were in the highly unbalanced colonial trading system that survived the demise of the colonial era. This continued to ensure that the Global North maintained its substantial economic advantage through favourable terms of trade maintained by quotas, tariffs, value added taxes and other means.

Thus, there have been more than three centuries of exploitation, first through slavery and then by persistent trading advantages and wealth extraction from colonies and former colonies.

Then came that global shock of the 1973–4 oil price rises and a parallel boom in commodity prices neatly coinciding with the emergence into the economic limelight of neoliberal thinking. By the mid-1970s numerous think tanks were pursuing the application of the neoliberal approach and there are now around five hundred such centres across the world, loosely associated with the Atlas Network[11] and often supported generously, if opaquely, by rich individuals and foundations.

At the base of neoliberalism is the belief that successful shareholder capitalism is best rooted in competition rather than cooperation. A mixed economy that has private and state-owned elements is, in this view, unacceptable and is far less efficient than a free market system with minimal government interference and regulation. Allowed a free rein, a properly free market economy will produce plenty of winners and generate much wealth. It will also end up with many losers. Indeed, inequality is essential to the functioning of a successful market economy, necessarily spurring on losers to work harder. In theory, sufficient wealth supposedly trickling down from the much more successful rich to the rest will be just enough to prevent social unrest and worse.

There had long been an element of neoliberalism in mixed economy systems but the economic pressures after the 1973–4 oil price shock brought the neoliberal outlook centre stage by the early 1980s, helped by the election of the Thatcher government in the UK in 1979 and Ronald Reagan in the US the following year. The main element of the neoliberal approach is the prioritisation of private enterprise in place of state ownership, which should be kept to a minimum. This should be across the board and include not just core industries but utilities and health and social care systems. It should also extend to education and

---

11. The Atlas Network is a global network of more than 500 think tanks, based in Arlington, Virginia: https://www.atlasnetwork.org/

security. The taxation system should be structured to support the successful, thereby increasing their wealth and further encouraging others to compete. Labour rights should be minimised, with legally enforceable limits on strikes and other forms of industrial action. Above all, there should be a minimum of state regulation of financial affairs. Given this list of ingredients, with some states already further down the neoliberal path than others, incoming governments would vary in the changes they sought.

Reagan and Thatcher

With Reagan in the US, for example, where there were already high levels of privatisation, including health, the emphasis was on tax reforms to aid success as well as further deregulation of the financial system. Thus, an early action by the Reagan administration was the Garn–St Germain Depository Institutions Act of 1982,[12] effectively reversing key elements of Roosevelt's 'New Deal' Glass–Steagall Act of 1933. The Reagan changes gave the banking system greater freedom from regulation and the tax reforms were mainly concessions aimed at the wealthy, exacerbating disparities in wealth.

The UK differed from the US in having higher existing levels of state ownership, so there was much more to do. The Thatcher government was helped by the once-in-a-lifetime bonanza of North Sea oil and gas, which made it possible to fund high levels of unemployment, at least for a few years. The radical changes that the Thatcher government brought in probably couldn't have been implemented without this lucky coincidence. Trade union power was systematically weakened by numerous government actions, and union membership decreased markedly as large-scale privatisation proceeded apace. Water and gas utilities

---

12. The Garn–St Germain Depository Institutions Act is not exactly one of the best-known acts of Congress, but it played an important role in deregulating a range of financial institutions in the early Reagan years. More than forty years on, quite a few political economists see this as one of the factors that made banks and other institutions more prone to risks, helping to set in motion the toxic-loans debacle of 2007–8 and the international financial crisis that followed.

were privatised, as were telecommunications, many prisons, and probation services.

One of the most substantial changes was the selling of council housing on a large scale; local councils were required to sell much of their stock and were not allowed to use most of the proceeds to build new housing. The biggest change of all was the so-called 'Big Bang' of 1986: the sudden deregulation of financial markets, including the privatisation of the London Stock Exchange.

The Thatcher decade and the eight years of Reagan's presidency were the powerhouse of the neoliberal transition, but many other states followed suit, if not all so enthusiastically. A crucial development across the Global South was the imposition of the 'Washington Consensus', a loose coalition of intergovernmental finance and trade bodies such as the International Monetary Fund (IMF) and World Bank. Financial support for specific states at a time of severe indebtedness was made dependent on implementing neoliberal policies. One mechanism was known as 'conditionality'. An urgently needed loan, for example, would be provided but only on condition that a state asset such as water was privatised or tax changes brought in that favoured the wealthier.

The market fundamentalism of the neoliberal model persists across the world, subject to some modification. It remains highly influential and is greatly enabled by those hundreds of well-funded think tanks. Although the UK Labour government of 1997–2010 was less aggressive in its approach than the Thatcher government it broadly bought into the model, perhaps its two biggest mistakes being support for private finance initiatives that have led to huge indebtedness in public bodies and, even worse, its failure to reverse the wholesale deregulation of the Big Bang. This made the 2008–9 financial crisis particularly severe for the UK, especially since it was followed by many years of Conservative governance that have reverted to type, starting with more than a decade of austerity that affected the poorest the most.

It is a pattern repeated in different ways worldwide, allowing several thousand billionaires and millions of other people who are seriously wealthy to be doing just fine and determined to maintain their wealth and status. Between 2020 and 2023, for example, the world's richest 1% captured nearly two-thirds of all new wealth globally.

Throughout history there have been the rich and powerful. In the European Middle Ages there was no shortage of lords with their castles. During the industrial revolutions even more wealth could be grabbed, first from slavery and later from coal, minerals, gems, spices and fine cloths. From the early twentieth century, for the best part of seventy years, the wealth–poverty divide did narrow a little in some Western states, but that came to an end with the neoliberal economic transformations of the 1980s. Take the UK once again as an example, where the concentration of massive wealth in a few hands is, to be frank, obscene. According to the *Sunday Times* Annual Rich List, in 2022 the wealth accumulation of just the richest five people was well over £100 billion.[13] Beyond them are many tens of thousands of people who are singularly rich and several million more who are nicely comfortable. All of this is in a state where life expectancy in the richest districts of individual cities can be a decade longer than the poorest areas and where food banks proliferate.

Of the global population of eight billion, perhaps six billion are relatively marginalised, two billion get by okay, a couple of hundred million are doing nicely, while just 1% are doing very well indeed and a million or so people are really coining it in. In the four years to January 2024, the world's five richest people (all men) doubled their fortunes to US$869 billion (£681.5 billion) while, over the same period, the world's poorest 60%, just short of five billion people, actually lost money.[14] The differences are so vast, thanks to the impact of the bitterly competitive neoliberal ideology, that very few people can even begin to get their heads around what these figures mean.

13. 'Rich List 2022', *Sunday Times Magazine*, 22 May 2022.
14. Rupert Neate, 'World's Five Richest Men Double Their Money as Poorest Get Poorer', *The Guardian*, 15 January 2024, https://www.theguardian.com/inequality/2024/jan/15/worlds-five-richest-men-double-their-money-as-poorest-get-poorer

One way is to see what a very modest wealth tax might do. In May 2023, three UK-based NGOs – Tax Justice UK, the Economic Change Unit and the New Economics Foundation[15] – assessed what sort of revenue would be raised from a modest 2% wealth tax on the UK's 350 richest families, the tax being on assets greater than £10 billion. It came to £22 billion each year. Given the rate at which these families' wealth was accumulating, for most of them there might not be any net loss; they just wouldn't get richer at quite the rate they had been doing before. Such is the nature of the world's crazy monetary system.

One of the UK's leading thinkers in the new field of international political economy (IPE), Professor Susan Strange, is considered by many to have virtually invented IPE and wrote many books, including key texts used by generations of students. Two of the best were the appropriately named *Casino Capitalism* (1988) and *Mad Money* (1998). The second, in particular, was uncomfortably accurate in its analysis of the faults of the system that eventually led to the 2007–8 financial meltdown. Sadly, Strange died in 1998 shortly after the publication of that book.

There is one little-recognised but important point to add here. Thanks to one of the relative successes across the Global South in recent decades, there have been impressive achievements in education systems and literacy, and because of this many of the billions of people who live in those countries are far more aware of their circumstances than their compatriots half a century ago. In the UK four decades or so ago, the phrase 'the revolution of rising expectations' was popular among social commentators. People may have been hard up, but life was getting better for everyone. Today, what is more likely is a 'revolution of frustrated expectations' as many millions of people find themselves sidelined and left with few if any prospects of a better life. To make matters worse, this is in a world facing the threat of climate breakdown. It is the combination of the two – environmental limits and a deeply

---

15. Tax Justice Network, https://taxjustice.net/; Economic Change Unit, https://www.econchange.org/; New Economics Foundation, https://neweconomics.org/

divided world – that makes for instability and the risk of violence stemming from resentment and anger.

And, on top of that, there is the unexpected.

A bug in the system

Time for a brief but relevant digression.

In August 2018 the UK government published a national biosecurity strategy, the outcome of a considered analysis of the risk of new pandemics and how to respond. It was an expert-led piece of work that was one of the factors that meant that the UK, along with the US, was considered one of the best-equipped countries in its ability to respond to a pandemic. However, when the COVID-19 pandemic got into its stride eighteen months later, the UK turned out to be one of the worst responders across the Global North, especially through being persistently late in taking expert advice. Why this was the case has much to do with the neoliberal mindset that then dominated government policy.

Precise dates are important here. The recognition of a serious new health problem originating in China was already present at the end of December 2019 in East Asia; Taiwan and Hong Kong both brought in travel restrictions to control entry from the Chinese city of Wuhan, the seat of the outbreak. The UK government was not even made aware of the issue until 3 January 2020 and not until 27 January was a meeting of the UK government's emergency committee, COBRA, called to discuss the problem. By then the highly infectious virus had spread from China to Thailand, Japan and South Korea and there were already close to a thousand cases in China, where the government had ordered a complete lockdown of Wuhan province, including the city of Wuhan with its population of over eight million.[16]

---

16. Paul Rogers, 'Early warning of biosecurity incidents', written evidence on the COVID-19 pandemic to the House of Commons Select Committee on Defence, 14 February 2021, https://committees.parliament.uk/writtenevidence/22663/html/

Despite the concern of most public health and epidemiology specialists, Boris Johnson's government showed little concern about the problem. Johnson did not even attend, let alone chair, the COBRA session. Instead, he made it crystal clear that this was simply not a problem when he delivered his first post-Brexit speech in Greenwich on 3 February, included a remarkable passage about the burgeoning pandemic:

We are starting to hear some bizarre autarkic rhetoric, when barriers are going up, and when there is a risk that new diseases such as coronavirus will trigger a panic and a desire for market segregation that go beyond what is medically rational to the point of doing real and unnecessary economic damage, then at that moment humanity needs some government somewhere that is willing at least to make the case powerfully for freedom of exchange, some country ready to take off its Clark Kent spectacles and leap into the phone booth and emerge with its cloak flowing as the supercharged champion of the right of the populations of the earth to buy and sell freely among each other. And here in Greenwich in the first week of February 2020, I can tell you in all humility that the UK is ready for that role.[17]

The message was blunt, that market fundamentalism came first, and this was not a place for government to intervene. Johnson disappeared just after the speech for a ten-day break, his second holiday in eight weeks, and failed to attend any of the next four COBRA meetings as the epidemic rapidly expanded its reach. Given the view expressed by Johnson at Greenwich, the government strongly resisted calls for a national lockdown and was supported in this by most national newspapers. Over the following two years COVID-19 killed 228,000 people in the UK, one of the worst results, relative to the size of population, of any country in the world.

---

17. Boris Johnson, 'PM Speech in Greenwich', 3 February 2020, https://www.gov.uk/government/speeches/pm-speech-in-greenwich-3-february-2020

In global terms the progress of the pandemic showed up the lack of intergovernmental responsibility, especially concerning what was termed 'vaccination nationalism', whereby more powerful states with money to spend looked to prioritise their own populations even though everyone would benefit from vaccinating those in the highest areas of COVID-19 incidence. As a direct consequence of the pandemic, share markets were far more volatile than usual and this was one area where rich individuals and especially hedge funds could reap handsome rewards. The peak period of market instability was the three months from April to July 2020; in that short period the world's 2,189 dollar billionaires increased their wealth by an extraordinary 27.5%. This came on top of a 70% rise over the previous three years. For the world's rich, COVID-19 was very good for business and their own wealth.[18]

Oxfam's annual global wealth assessment published early in 2021 reported that in the first year of the pandemic the combined wealth of the world's ten richest people, all men, increased by US$540 billion – calculated to be enough to pay for COVID-19 vaccination for the world's eight billion people and to prevent anyone from falling into poverty through the impact of the virus.

Not fit for purpose

What all this points to is that the world's dominant economic model is terribly ill suited to responding to global challenges that need close intergovernmental cooperation. COVID-19 is a recent example and we are now faced with the historically unique problem of accelerating climate breakdown. The latter requires sustained, rapid and radical action by governments and peoples all working together across the world to accomplish revolutionary changes of behaviour over the next decade. To judge by current experience, that is simply not happening and the risk is rising

---

18. Rupert Neate, 'Billionaires' wealth rises to $10.2 trillion amid Covid crisis', *The Guardian*, 7 October 2020; Sam Jones and Valentina Romei, 'Pandemic Makes the World's Billionaires – and their Advisors – Even Richer', *Financial Times*, 23 October 2020.

that states will look to protect their own. Indeed, they are already doing so, and one example is staring us in the face.

One of the well-nigh certain effects of climate breakdown will be huge increases in migration as desperate people try to move to safer places. There has already been an increase in such movements, some owing to climatic changes and others, more commonly so far, because of war, persecution or poverty. Some assessments of the impact of climate breakdown suggest that the increase in migratory pressures could be up to tenfold what is being experienced at present.

The migration that is already happening, though, has brought about thoroughly callous attitudes to people desperately needing help, thousands having been left to drown in the Mediterranean and the English Channel. The UK is an example of what could happen on a much larger scale. The UK population is ageing; a sustained increase in the numbers of younger people is needed in order to fill the gaps in the labour force. Instead, politicians, especially but not only of the far right, depict migrants and asylum-seekers as a 'threat' and even as 'invaders', not as people who combine an ability to plug that gap with a desperate need to escape their home countries.

If that is what we have now, then borders will harden substantially as migration pressures rise. Barriers to movement are being strengthened. Trump wanted a barrier all the way along the US border with Mexico, and elsewhere even more extreme measures are being adopted. An appalling example is the experience of refugees from war-torn parts of Ethiopia who, having managed to cross Somalia and get across the Red Sea to Yemen, then try to get into Saudi Arabia, only to be shot in cold blood by Saudi border guards.

These, and other examples, are part of the common experience of desperate asylum-seekers and migrants today. Assuring security by force will become the order of the day. When push comes to shove, it will be military force that is turned to. This is one reason why we must recognise the nature of military systems and the role they are likely to play in keeping the richer communities safe and secure.

CHAPTER THREE

Now Thrive the Armourers

Military-industrial complexes, their culture, how they work and how they limit new thinking on insecurity

In August 2023, eighteen months into Russia's disastrous invasion of Ukraine, with a violent stalemate and no prospect of an end to war, Western arms corporations were reporting full order books and sharp increases in their share prices. The UK-based BAE Systems saw its share price go up 70% from before the conflict, Sweden's Saab saw a doubling over the same period, and Germany's largest armourer, Rheinmetall, saw its share price treble. 'Now thrive the armourers' was very much the order of the day as military budgets surged across Europe by 13% in one year. The worldwide increase of 3.7% took the world total to over US$2 trillion spent on the military in a single year.

Meanwhile, a US government assessment in late August 2023 put the total number of people killed or injured in the Ukraine conflict at half a million. For the Russians the numbers were 120,000 dead and 170,000–180,000 injured and for the Ukrainians close to 70,000 killed and 100,000–120,000 injured. The Ukrainian deaths already exceed all US combat deaths for the whole of the eleven-year Vietnam War.

Then came the war in Gaza, where Israel reacted with huge force to the grievous Hamas attack of 7 October when 1,200 Israelis were killed and more than 240 were taken hostage. In the first three months after the attack, Israel used massive force to try to destroy Hamas, killing twenty-five thousand Gazans, including more than ten thousand children, wounding over fifty thousand people and reducing much of Gaza to rubble. Paralleling this was an arms bonanza in the wider region. Israel received billions of dollars' worth of new bombs and missiles, other states were quickly upping their arms imports, the salespeople were celebrating the success of some of the new weapons, and the armourers were thriving even more.

Audiences across the Western world have seen the impact of war at close quarters to a greater degree in 2022–4 than during the two decades of the War on Terror, even with the massive destruction that wrought in Afghanistan, Iraq, Libya and elsewhere. Cities such as Fallujah, Raqqa and Ramadi suffered widespread destruction, the old city of Mosul was reduced to rubble, and Iraq alone lost around 200,000 civilians. That all had some impact on Western public opinion but did not bring the reality of intense aerial bombardment home to people to anything like the same extent of Ukraine and Gaza despite the appalling and long-lasting human consequences of those earlier wars.

According to an independent analysis by the Costs of War Programme at Brown University in the United States, by mid-2023 over 940,000 people had died in the post-9/11 wars as a result of direct war violence and an estimated 3.6 to 3.8 million people had died indirectly, about thirty-eight million people were displaced and the total cost of the conflicts was US$8 trillion.[19] When the devastation is factored into those figures, the 'plague on both your houses' response to the US-led War on Terror across the Global South begins to become understandable.

There are strong arguments that the war in Iraq was illegal, being fought on the false premise of Iraq's arsenal of weapons of mass destruction which did not even exist. And those few analysts who argued that going to war in Afghanistan after 9/11 would be a huge error were proved right. Instead, the Al-Qaeda leadership should have been seen as perpetrators of mass transnational homicide and brought to trial, however long that took.

Two decades later, with the Taliban in full control of Afghanistan and with paramilitaries linked to ISIS (Islamic State

---

19. https://www.brown.edu/news/2021-09-01/costsofwar

of Iraq and Syria) and Al-Qaeda still active across the Middle East and South Asia and expanding their activities in the Sahel and Central Africa, things look different. The military 'solution' of the War on Terror seems much more of a failure. Although a non-military response never looked likely at the time, it certainly makes much more sense now.

The failed wars in Afghanistan, Iraq and Libya are little talked about in polite military circles and Putin's assault in Ukraine seems welcome in NATO military systems as a return to a more traditional kind of war. But that isn't good enough. Instead, we must rethink what we mean by 'security'. A good starting point is to remind ourselves about current military culture, not least because it seems so comprehensively unsuited to the greatest challenges to human wellbeing, especially the marginalisation of billions of people and the vast challenge of climate breakdown. Military systems seem irrelevant except where they are no more than a desperate attempt to maintain control of a disrupted world system. If we are going to get to grips with all this, a good place to start is the phenomenon often referred to as the 'military–industrial complex'.

Complex in name and nature

All states that have substantial armed forces have such a complex and they have considerable power, whether the states are organised as democracies, autocracies or hybrids. There are many cross-state connections, especially in international military alliances such as NATO, that give the complexes even more power. Some military–industrial complexes, such as those in the US, UK, France, Russia and increasingly China, have long histories of manufacturing and exporting armaments. A few, such as Sweden and Switzerland, have security postures that are primarily defensive while maintaining substantial arms industries with thriving export profiles.

The UK, as a middle power still riddled with pretensions of greatness, has a security complex with most of the features seen elsewhere and can serve as an example for many. At its centre is a combination of the military, the civil service and the corporations, the latter comprising arms manufacturers and also private military companies and intelligence outfits. Although the military will see their role as 'defenders of the realm', career prospects loom large within them, as they do in the civil service and the corporations.

In the business sector and especially at the senior corporate level, the overarching concern is profitability within a mainly shareholder capitalist system. Corporate leaders have the added attraction of a generous bonus culture so often linked to profitability in a very profitable industry that is aided by two trends. First, in many states there are monopolies of production for submarines, large surface warships, main battle tanks, strike aircraft and other major items. Second, in the past sixty years there have been numerous mergers and takeovers, consolidating the industry into fewer corporations. Worldwide, this means that a handful of corporations wield huge lobbying power and influence. Moreover, the likes of Boeing, Lockheed Martin and BAE Systems are multinational corporations with subsidiaries and agents in scores of countries.

Beyond this core of armed forces, private contractors, civil service and arms companies are the intelligence agencies, consultancies, think tanks and universities. There are also the trade unions concerned with their members' interests, although these may well include a concern to diversify out of military production. In the UK there has long been a cross-party assessment rooted in the requirement for a strong military capability that includes nuclear weapons. Over the last twenty years Britain has also put more resources into the capacity to deploy military force as far as the Pacific, part of a near desperate and expensive effort to be a major power on the world stage. Since the Russian invasion of Ukraine, the UK has been one of many countries that plan to increase their military budget towards 2.5% of gross national product and quite possibly higher.

Neoliberal economics and deep privatisation also have an impact on the military. Mercenaries have been for hire throughout the ages, but the private contractor is now a commercial agent of the state for the conduct of expeditionary operations across an expanded battlespace. Private military and security companies (PMSCs) function as force multipliers that enhance the state's ability to fight wars remotely. Contractors allow states to achieve military objectives overseas with little or no transparency, plausible deniability and potentially lower political costs. Satellite technology and high-tech computerised remote warfare systems enable invisible killing ('unmanned warfare') unless they are monitored, probed and held to account.

Within the complex there is continual interchange. Military officers are seconded to corporations, as are senior civil servants, and there is movement the other way. Universities take on military and corporate staff, as do think tanks. Corporations are particularly keen to integrate with both senior military officers and civil servants if they are concerned with weapons research, development and especially procurement. When such people are heading for retirement, they are attractive to the corporate sector and will themselves look towards well-paid advisory posts and consultancies, the most senior of them to directorships. This revolving door system is not restricted to the military and civil service; former and serving politicians regularly find lucrative posts to supplement their income.

Although the structure of the complex – military, civil service, corporations and all the other groups – needs to be understood, just as important is the culture that permeates the entire system. In the UK, the Rethinking Security group identifies this culture as a thoroughly outmoded if deeply embedded narrative, in which security policy:[20]

- privileges UK national security as always coming first, superseding other needs, rather than recognising security as a common value to which all people have equal claim;

---

20. The following paragraphs on rethinking security draw heavily on work that originated with the Ammerdown Conversation and its development into the Rethinking Security group, https://rethinkingsecurity.org.uk/. See, in particular, this analysis of what a new approach to security might mean: Ammerdown Group, *Rethinking Security: A Discussion Paper*, 2016, https://www.researchgate.net/publication/318129168_Rethinking_security_A_discussion_paper

- aims to advance 'national interests' defined by the political establishment, including corporate business interests and UK 'world power' status, and therefore dissociates the practice of security from the needs of people in their communities;
- assumes a short-term outlook and presents physical threats of violence as the main risks, largely overlooking long-term drivers of insecurity such as climate breakdown;
- responds by exerting control over the strategic environment, concentrating on offensive military capabilities, transnational alliances, and restrictions on civil liberties.

This culture is typically dominated by a relatively small group drawn from a social elite, with a disproportionate influence from business interests, especially the arms industries. It is set in its ways, and this leads to difficulty in recognising any need for change, still less any alternative concepts of security. Furthermore, there is a preference for values associated with hegemonic masculinity, which all too often reduces thinking to a calculus of threats and coercive responses with little or no concern for social and ecological elements of security.

It is a mistake to think that people in the military–industrial complex are inevitably gung-ho warmongers. Some certainly are, but quite a few senior officers in the armed forces take a broad view of international relations, and some certainly see the dangers of collective challenges such as climate breakdown. For all of them, though, the main function of the armed forces is the defence of the state; this means that they look to the consequences rather than the causes of climate breakdown and do their best to minimise those impacts. It is for politicians and others to consider the possibility of preventing climate breakdown in the first place. Even those few in the military who see climate breakdown as a danger that must be prevented before it gets out of hand rarely speak truth to power, though there are notable exceptions if mostly among the recently retired.

Similarly, within the military–industrial complexes of the nuclear armed powers, few people within the system question the reasons for retaining nuclear weapons. Just nine countries possess them: the US, Russia, France, China, the UK, Israel, Pakistan, India and North Korea. Four countries have given them up in recent decades: South Africa, Belarus, Ukraine and Kazakhstan. World nuclear arsenals peaked at over seventy thousand warheads in the 1980s; since it would only take a dozen nuclear weapons to wreck a country, this was an utterly ludicrous degree of overkill.

Since the Cold War total nuclear arsenals have come down to around eight thousand, which is still massive, and all the nuclear weapon states are modernising their arsenals. Some, including the UK and China, are even increasing the size of their arsenal. Although the UN has agreed the Treaty on the Prohibition of Nuclear Weapons, no nuclear weapons power has signed up to it so far. Many other states have done so, 93 of them by late 2023, of which 69 have ratified it into law, but there is still a very long way to go to achieve a nuclear-free world.

There is a Chemical Weapons Convention which has powers of inspection and most of the huge chemical weapon arsenals of the Cold War era have been destroyed. The Biological and Toxin Weapons Convention, though, does not have an inspection procedure. Given the potential to produce bioweapons tailored to specific tasks, this marks a continuing failure of international arms control. Weapons of mass destruction are still with us after numerous failures of attempts at arms control, and this is yet another indicator of the power of the military–industrial complex.

In sum, then, when assessing the overall importance of the military-industrial complex to a state's security posture, four elements should be recognised. First, an embedded culture sees military force as the primary response to perceived security threats. Second, the arms industry tends to be highly profitable, as well as having plenty of scope for bribery, aka 'commission'. Third, any questioning of the system is easily dismissed as defeatist, unpatriotic or even a potential security threat. Fourth, the system needs wars in order to thrive.

Furthermore, the complexes themselves are evolving, not least as new forms of warfare are developed. In the early 2020s, autonomous systems such as armed drones really came to the fore, greatly increasing the potential for irregular warfare, especially when cheap expandable drones can be mass produced; and we are still in the early stages of using artificial intelligence. There are valid arguments that the term 'military–industrial complex' fails to describe the nature of the beast. In 2019, a US analyst, Daniel Wirls, put it this way:

> We used to call the nexus of private interests and national defense the 'military–industrial complex.' But that Cold War term no longer fits. 'Industrial' does not capture the breadth of the activities involved. And 'military' fails to describe the range of government policies and interests implicated. Over the past two decades we've seen transformations that include new government reliance on private security firms, revolutions in digital technology, a post-9/11 surge in the number of veterans, and the creation of the Department of Homeland Security (DHS). What we have now could be called a 'National Security Corporate Complex.'[21]

To put it crudely, a military system at its worst may be described as a 'war-promoting hydra'. When it comes to the profitability of armaments production, which can make up as much as half of all military spending, an ideal war is one in which it is possible to arm both sides, that lasts a long time and that does not directly involve the militaries of the country providing the armaments. A long-lasting violent stalemate makes for a highly profitable business environment. A cynical view, maybe, but remember the value of the conflict in Ukraine to those arms corporations and remember how just the first few weeks of Israel's war in Gaza boosted arms sales right across the Middle East. Don't forget that the world's military complexes *need* arms races and wars in order to thrive and that most such complexes are rooted in shareholder capitalist systems.

---

21. Daniel Wirls, 'Eisenhower Called It the "Military–Industrial Complex". It's Vastly Bigger Now', Washington Post, 26 June 2019.

CHAPTER FOUR

So, Where are We Now?

The current predicament, prospects for positive changes and whether they can come fast enough; achieving rapid decarbonisation, a reformed economy and rethinking security; how to act to help ensure we succeed

There are plenty of other challenges, including new pandemics, artificial intelligence, nano-weapons and remote warfare, but the argument put here is that three stand out above all the others: environmental limits, deep socioeconomic divisions with consequent mass marginalisation, and a military culture that relies on vigorous and typically violent responses to security challenges. Those last two, economy and security, are long term while also requiring immediate responses, but the environmental issues are also having a rapidly accelerating impact, and so an effective response requires understanding how all three interconnect.

The three mega-trends intersect in dynamic, harsh ways. For example, climate change and environmental degradation undermine global agricultural production and livelihoods, resulting in food insecurity; famine for some, higher prices for others. Concerns are also rising over water usage and supply. Impacts fall heavily on subsistence farmers, pastoralists and fishing people in the Global South; increased poverty and competition for resources create pressures and vulnerabilities that lead to forced migration or exploitation by armed groups or elites. Localised conflicts and rebellion bring reactions and wars that fuel demand for armaments and further divide and undermine whole populations, fuelled by politics of desperation, greed and the abuse of power. It is an insecurity trap of immense proportions.

The public perception of climate breakdown in many parts of the world has changed from an issue for the future to a far more immediate concern. Such an extraordinary range of droughts, floods and intense heatwaves have been seen in so many parts of the world that it is difficult to ignore the reality that this global problem is immediate, not something a decade or more down the line. The response must be well underway by 2030 but there is little evidence of any fundamental shift in national or intergovernmental policies; there is, instead, more of a make do and mend attitude. A few states are at last getting serious, some politicians do understand what needs to be done, but they too are few and time is short.

It is therefore helpful to get a sense of where we will be by 2030 if there is no significant change from the current slow rate of response and, on the other hand, where we will be if there is a more radical and rapid response. This may be disconcerting and depressing, but hang on, there are plenty of positive aspects to consider a few pages further on.

Glowering planet

Let us assume that over the next few years through to 2030 there will be very little change in the level of response to climate breakdown. The current concentration of carbon dioxide in the atmosphere is 412 parts per million (ppm), which is 47% higher than it was at the start of the industrial age, when the concentration is reckoned to have been 280 ppm. Forty years ago, climate scientists talked of limiting the rise to 350 ppm but by 2000 it was already up to 370 ppm. A good aim now would still be to get back to around 350 ppm but that would require an annual decrease in emissions of at least 10% for many years, whereas, at present, even with all the publicity and the movement to renewables, the carbon dioxide in the atmosphere is still increasing.

On this basis, the recent experience of heat domes, droughts, floods and storms will get decidedly worse, more parts of the world will see crop yields diminish, malnutrition and starvation will increase and many more people will try to migrate to those countries where they have a better prospect of a half-decent life. In the coming years the concentration of wealth will intensify, increasing the rich–poor division, if little is done to address the failing neoliberal economic system.

Those who 'have', or think they 'have', will be even keener to maintain their own wealth and ensure their own security, and right-wing populist politics will become much more popular, right across Europe and North America. The attitude to migration will harden even further into the 'close the castle gates' stance. As borders are made more secure, a major function of military and police forces will be to keep out the unwanted.

In other words, what we already see before us will intensify, while the powerful and exceptionally well-funded fossil carbon industries will make as much money as they possibly can for as long as they possibly can. Sometime, likely in the early 2030s but quite possibly sooner, the proverbial will hit the fan. Catastrophes will directly affect some of the richest states; for example, a sudden intense heat dome may affect a major city and kill many thousands within a couple of days. There may be a Category Six hurricane with an impact similar to or much worse than the Derna disaster in Libya in 2023 but this time affecting a city in Europe or North America. Such an event may finally tip the balance in favour of rapid and radical economic decarbonisation. This will have become unavoidable but will be decidedly more difficult, both politically and economically, because of the decades of failure to face up to what needs to be done.

There is a further problem that is well-nigh certain to emerge. When and where are impossible to predict, but the signs are already there. This is the issue of 'revolts from the margins'. Back in the 1990s, a few security analysts were pointing to the risk posed by such revolts, owing to an innate vulnerability of modern urban-industrial societies to disruption. Such fears were almost entirely dismissed, even when there were specific warnings of attacks on major urban targets such as financial, military or business centres. That changed after the experience of 9/11, but still did not extend to trying to recognise what might be happening. *Losing Control*, which I wrote in the late 1990s, put it this way:

> *What should be expected is that new social movements will develop that are essentially anti-elite in nature and will draw their support from people, especially men, on the margins. In different contexts and circumstances, they may have their roots in political ideologies, religious beliefs, ethnic, nationalist or cultural identities, or a complex combination of several of these. They may be focused on individuals or groups, but the most common feature is an opposition to existing centres of power ... What can be said is that, on present trends, anti-elite action will be a core feature of the next 30 years – not so much a clash of civilisations, more an age of insurgencies.*

What went on to happen in Afghanistan, Iraq, the Sahel and elsewhere in the ensuing decades followed that thinking but much of it was linked specifically to the US-led post-9/11 War on Terror and often involved a radical Islamist element with a willingness to die for their beliefs. More than two decades later, the growing impact of climate breakdown alongside people's existing marginalisation will lead to diverse political, ethnic, nationalist and other drivers of action. Where and when may be difficult to predict but as a long-term trend it seems close to inevitable, at least on the basis of current behaviour.

One widespread concern is far-right populism, especially in enabling ambitious politicians to latch on to the issue of migration even before the pressures to move become greatly exacerbated by climate breakdown. It is not easy to get a handle of this because the growth of hard-right populism is highly variable. Throughout the past seventy years there have been waves of far-right populism, many influencing political moods and some even gaining control of governments. There have also been responses going the other way. In the early 1970s autocratic far-right governments were in control in Spain, Portugal and Greece but all these had gone before the end of the decade. In addition, until 1989 large parts of Eastern Europe were dominated by the Soviet Union, but that came apart in barely a year, under the pressure of numerous citizen movements. More recently, the Trump experience has been salutary, as has Bolsonaro's regime in Brazil, and both Putin and Xi Jinping have favoured rigid control of their respective states.

An enduring concern is the way that misinformation can have a rapid and pervasive impact, utilising multiple media outlets and often deliberately fostering extreme views. Time and again the focus is on 'the other', especially immigrants, seen as a threat. Immigrants serve the purpose of providing a common enemy responsible for many different problems and of enabling elite power centres to divert attention, especially from the almost unbelievable accumulation of wealth and power of those in control. Brooks's 'crowded glowering planet' with 'wealth buttressed by stark force' seems all too plausible. Perhaps we are already more than halfway there.

Is transformation possible?

Now let us assume that in the late 2020s the global attitude to climate breakdown does change and that towards the end of the decade carbon emissions first plateau and then actually start to decrease. A 10% decrease per annum up to 2030 is hoping for a lot. Even so, the combination of public pressure, the low cost of renewable energy compared with fossil carbon sources, some effective political and ethical leadership and the impact of catastrophic events could all be having an effect.

Over that 2025–30 period, though, the beginnings of a reversal will not be enough to halt the effects of the carbon dioxide that is already in the atmosphere. Carbon dioxide's presence in the atmosphere is part of a wider biogeochemical cycle. The rate that this cycle turns is slow, which means that carbon dioxide released into the atmosphere from coal, gas, oil and wood combustion will be there for up to thirty years. This means that even after we start to reverse the current trend of increasing carbon dioxide levels it will take more than a decade before the decrease is significant.

The consequence is that modest gains will still mean exceptional weather-based catastrophes, rising sea level, decreases in food production, dangerous new disease patterns and much political and social unrest. Huge expenditure will still be required to improve resilience, manage large-scale migration and change thinking on security by curbing the war-promoting hydras of the military–industrial complex. That all means that the competitive environment of the neoliberal market fundamentalist economic model must be challenged. Climate breakdown means that an economic model rooted in competition cannot cope with the need for cooperation at every level from neighbourhoods right through to intergovernmental action.

How fast, and how can it be done?

Things must change far faster than is widely recognised. To talk of getting to net zero emissions by 2050 is plain nonsense. It must be a worldwide aim for 2040 at the latest and preferably by 2035, but a uniform expectation of reduction across the world would be unfair on the world's weaker economies, primarily in the Global South. The countries of the Global North must bring their emissions down very much faster than currently planned, and they must become far more energy efficient; but an even bigger issue is the critical need to provide substantial financial support for countries in the Global South to make the jump to a post-carbon era of renewable energy resources combined with highly efficient energy conservation.

What we are looking at is a third revolution in human organisation and behaviour every bit as substantial as the first two. Number one was the Neolithic transition from hunting-gathering to farming which began ten thousand years ago, greatly increasing the capacity of the land to support people and making towns and cities possible. The second transition is far more recent – the three-centuries-long industrial revolution that is having such a dangerous environmental impact. The third transition, to a sustainable global system, is essential yet contains a hidden but giant problem. The main thrust of the Neolithic transition was spread over several millennia. The industrial revolution has been underway for three centuries and is still a work in progress. The third transition has to happen very much faster.

To prevent systemic climate breakdown and unbearable catastrophes, we need to achieve radical change almost beyond comprehension within a couple of decades, and the serious beginnings of that change by 2030. It can be done, just, and a key to this is to recognise the sheer extent of the challenge while simultaneously knowing just how quickly changes can be made in the face of a clear and present danger.

This is one reason why it was worth the digression into the COVID-19 pandemic a few pages ago. COVID-19 is still very much around, four years after the initial outbreak, and there may yet be further serious waves. The intergovernmental cooperation should have been far better in many respects, though there were some high points, including the impressive speed of developing vaccines. The pandemic spread rapidly and caught far too many states by surprise; little international leadership was shown by any major political figure.

The climate crisis is different in that it is happening more slowly, but it is obvious that it is happening now and needs radical and rapid action well in advance of the main impact. Such action will be difficult to pull off, but states and even interstate organisations can react quickly at times. The problem is that such rapid responses all too often happen because of a direct threat from another state or alliance, the response taking the form of some kind of war mobilisation for which plans will exist and have even been rehearsed.

Wars are regularly planned and prepared for, but that doesn't mean that the climate breakdown challenge is a lost cause. What it does mean is that the best way of meeting it is through radical decarbonisation while avoiding a security approach rooted in military answers to rising problems like mass migration. The response must also face down an economic system that depends too much on an unrestricted free market ideology concerned with short-term gain and will not therefore respond at anything like the speed required.

Going green, with some red thrown in

So how might it happen? And how might an individual state change? Take the UK for example. It is a middle-ranking state even if it still thinks it is 'great', but it has plenty of unrealised potential for renewables, has a history of social welfare reforms from the early post-war era and is on its way to being a cosmopolitan state, even if it still has some way to go with that. On the basis of our breaking down the challenge into environment, economy and security, here are some suggestions. Far from constituting a blueprint, they may help to give a sense of changed direction that will apply in different ways to every state.

Start with a misunderstanding. The UK government prides itself on being ahead of the game in weaning its economy off fossil carbon as its primary energy source. If you go back to the 1990s, there seems some truth in this, until you examine the motivations and methods of the UK's policies. In the 1990s and early 2000s the UK did move away from coal as a primary source for electricity generation, in favour of gas-fired power stations, and so carbon emissions did fall. The main motivation was to replace old coal-fired power plants with more efficient gas-fired power plants using gas mainly from the North Sea. It had precious little to do with preventing climate breakdown.

Furthermore, the de-industrialisation of the Thatcher era meant that far more goods bought in the UK were manufactured in China, Malaysia, India, Bangladesh and other states with lower labour costs, while the UK built up its financial services industries instead. By outsourcing production it also outsourced the carbon emissions, so China and other states became responsible for a large part of the UK's carbon output.

Add that into the country's carbon budget and you get a very different but conveniently ignored picture. The oft-repeated claim that the UK has massively reduced emissions in its laudable aim to counter climate breakdown is largely accounted for by the 'dash for gas' because gas was cheaper, and outsourcing because that too was cheaper. They together make up much more than half of the reduction, but neither of them was motivated by the risk of climate breakdown.

Towards the end of the last Labour government in 2010, some initial steps were taken, notably the 2008 Climate Change Act that established the statutory Committee on Climate Change setting a legally binding target on greenhouse gas emissions. The push to some action on decarbonisation was largely maintained by the Conservative/Liberal Democrat coalition government of 2010–15, primarily because the Liberal Democrats insisting on meeting existing commitments. When Conservative ministers spoke in private to the fossil carbon industries, as I once heard them do, they made it abundantly clear that they were just going through the motions because of their annoying coalition partners.

When the Conservatives gained an overall majority in the 2015 election, large parts of the green agenda were simply dropped, including a requirement for much higher energy conservation standards for new housing. Financial support for domestic photovoltaic-generated electricity was drastically reduced and generous subsidies for oil and gas continued. Obstacles were even put in the way of new onshore wind power projects, even though they would produce much cheaper electricity. The UK did make some further progress in control of carbon emissions through to the early 2020s, but largely because both solar and offshore wind power were becoming seriously profitable.

Given the UK's huge renewable energy resources, what could really be done in a multi-year programme of transition? The transition would benefit hugely from a publicly owned energy network focused as much on energy conservation as on expanding the use of renewable resources. A national warm homes scheme could aim to see every home highly insulated well within a decade. That alone would make a substantial dent in energy requirements while meeting head-on the problem of fuel poverty as well as providing hundreds of thousands of new jobs. All new housing should be built to a much higher standard of energy efficiency and most should routinely have solar photovoltaic panels fitted.

Throughout the economy there should be a programme matching the warm homes transition but for the workplace, whether office, retail premises or factory floor. It should be the norm for public buildings, factories, distribution centres and the rest to have high standards of energy conservation. Factories and public buildings should have photovoltaic arrays as a matter of course. All this will be paralleled by decreases in the cost of electricity in a publicly owned system that makes far greater use of cheaper renewables, with the two combined to reduce substantially the cost of living and working.

There should be a national programme of accelerated change in transport with heavy investment in nationalised rail and bus services, all electrified, and a speeding up of the move to electric cars and electric commercial vehicles right through to heavy goods vehicles, using a mix of fiscal controls and incentives to reduce costs. Priority should be given to public transport with much reduced fares, especially but not only in the larger population centres, where a subsidiary aim will be to improve air quality and hence the inhabitants' respiratory health.

A wide range of carbon reduction programmes across all the major sectors of society should work in parallel with a progressive restructuring of the food system which will include investment in a much-improved health education system. Air travel will be much reduced partly through increased surcharging, and airport expansion should stop. Roadbuilding will be much reduced with an emphasis on supporting public transport, cycling and walking. Internal-combustion-engine-powered vehicles will be seen as interesting museum pieces.

All these changes should be having an impact before 2030

as the UK moves towards a 10%+ per annum reduction in emissions. The entire process will involve much greater reliance on electricity as the main energy source for homes, work and industry. This will require a comprehensive speeding up of wind, wave and solar power use, partly funded by subsidies diverted from fossil fuels. Research and development of new systems will be aided by increased government funding. Promising areas include the new generation of high-power deep-water far-offshore wind turbines, hybrid perovskite/silicon photovoltaics and a range of energy storage systems. Given that the new generations of nuclear power plants produce electricity at three times the cost of renewables, even without factoring in the massive costs of cleanup, nuclear power will not be relevant.

Then there is the urgent need to cooperate with others of the richer states to provide serious funding for green transitions right across the Global South. If we know where to look, there is no shortage of funds. Just a 5% tax on oil and gas products would yield £158 billion globally each year and 0.1% on global financial services would yield a staggering £331 billion. That would not be enough to meet the total costs of anticipated loss and damage from climate breakdown or of empowering poorer countries across the Global South to move to renewable energy sources, but it would be a very welcome start.

Beyond all of this will be a progressive change in culture, aided by an evolving education system that will no doubt be reconfigured by the world's increasingly damaging experiences of extreme weather events. Above all, there will be changed attitudes to the current economic system and its extensive flaws that consistently militate against the green transition.

A reformed economy

When it comes to economic change, remember that the driving force of the neoliberal economic system is competition, not cooperation. There *must* be losers as well as winners and from this perspective it is useful to divide people into skivers and strivers, the former having themselves to blame for their position. In enabling the success of winners this is all part of the rotten system and ensures economic growth, combined with a tax system that favours the few, not the many. As we have seen, the intensity of neoliberal policies varies across countries, but most Western states have embraced neoliberalism and many states across the Global South have had little choice but to follow neoliberal orthodoxy because of the conditions frequently imposed in return for support from international organisations such as the IMF and the World Bank.

There was some moderating of the neoliberal approach in the UK under Tony Blair after 1997 but this was modest at best and many of the Thatcher government's policies were accepted, albeit with a welcome increase of public spending in two key areas – health and education. One major failure was to control the free market fundamentalism that reshaped the financial City of London before 1997 and culminated in the 2008 financial crash. From 2010 onwards, under the Conservatives, there was a return to fully fledged neoliberalism starting with more austerity.

On occasion this went too far even for the markets. In September 2022, Liz Truss's brief period as prime minister included a market fundamentalist budget that was dreamed up partly with London-based free-market think tanks. It was initially welcomed with open arms by government-supporting billionaire-owned newspapers: the *Daily Mail* headlined it, 'At Last! A *True* Tory Budget'. Within thirty-six hours, though, the stock markets gave a hugely negative verdict. The changes were going too far and too fast even for them, the government promptly U-turned and Truss was thrown to the wolves.

Major tax changes began under Margaret Thatcher after 1979 and the results, four decades later, have been huge benefits for the wealthy, trade union power severely curbed, numerous public assets sold off, low-cost social housing sidelined, public spending (especially on local authorities) reduced and, above all, the easing of regulatory oversight of banks and other financial institutions. Throughout the past four decades there have been groups proposing different ways forward. At the political level one major party briefly presented a challenge – the 2015–20 Labour party under Jeremy Corbyn. It came close to winning the 2017 general election on an unusually progressive economic manifesto, but he was then subject to bitter opposition from within the party as well as a media onslaught that persisted for the next three years.

Alternative economic models recognising the failures of neoliberalism have been developed in many countries, including Britain. Notable in Britain has been the work of the New Economics Foundation, mainly on the domestic economy, and Global Justice Now, on the global picture. The Ellen McCarthy Foundation has been prominent in developing the idea of the 'circular economy' and Kate Raworth's 'doughnut economics', which aims for everyone to have access to life's essentials within a system that does not exceed global ecological limits. A circular economy is a system of resource production and consumption that prioritises sharing, reusing, repairing, renewing and recycling existing materials and products as long as possible, rather than focusing on surplus or growth.

In whatever way we move on from the neoliberal failure, the actual process will need to be incremental and yet stimulate rapid change. In the UK an immediate move will be to restore public ownership of utilities, health and social care. Public funding of local politics needs to be increased and labour relations to be much improved. Above all, there needs to be action in three key areas: reform of financial regulation; a fair graduated tax system; and control of tax avoidance and evasion, including the elimination of tax havens. These measures will raise vast sums for new developments, especially investment in the transition to a low-carbon economy. Bear in mind, also, that shareholder capitalism, with all its failings, is not the only game in town. Cooperatives and mutuals may not yet be very significant in the UK, but across the Global South cooperatives are much more embedded, with 950 million members worldwide. They have plenty of potential for expansion in the UK.

Rethinking security

This brief summary is intended simply to point to alternative ways forward and to make clear that there really are other ways. The fact that a system is so resolutely set in its ways does not mean there can be no change. On the contrary, it really can be done. That need for change brings us to the question of what to do about the current approach to security, seen primarily as synonymous with defence and organised as an integrated military–industrial–technological complex. This understanding privileges national security over common values and advances 'the national interest', as motivated especially in the UK by the wish for world status and by a markedly business orientation. In short, it focuses on state-level security and the need to exert control over the strategic environment, this focus being dissociated from the needs of people in their communities. Its approach is essentially short term and is based on responding to threats as they present themselves rather than on countering the conditions that produce threats. Conflict prevention is rarely part of the culture. To make matters worse, the military–industrial complex is infused with the culture of hegemonic masculinity and is all too often abstracted from real-life impacts.

That whole approach must change. To say that is to state the obvious. The international order was hardly peaceful in the last century, but since 2001 there have been ever more failures of the conventional paradigm. Post-9/11 wars in Afghanistan and across the Middle East have been abject failures, in which four million people have died and tens of millions more have been uprooted. The COVID-19 pandemic has killed over twenty million people so far and has demonstrated the conspicuous failure of governments to work sufficiently together. The response to the risk of climate breakdown has so far been lamentable. In seeking a different paradigm, it is worth looking once again to the Rethinking Security group, which identifies security as having four elements:

- *Security as freedom.* Security may be understood as a shared freedom from fear and want, and the freedom to live in dignity. It implies social and ecological health rather than the absence of risk.
- *Security as a common right.* A commitment to commonality is imperative; security should not, and usually cannot, be gained by one group of people at others' expense. Thus, security rests on solidarity rather than dominance – in standing with others rather than against them.
- *Security as a patient practice.* Security grows or withers according to how inclusive and just a society is and how socially and ecologically responsible we its members are. It cannot be coerced into being.
- *Security as a shared responsibility.* Security is a common responsibility; its challenges belong to all of us. The continuing deterioration of security worldwide testifies against entrusting our common wellbeing to a self-selected group of powerful states.

This approach is so different from the norm that it will not take root overnight, but during the COVID-19 pandemic the notion of human security entered the public domain in real and dramatic ways. A nation's health is also part of its security, and one area of responsible governance is the wellbeing of citizens.

It is not difficult to envisage changes in existing paradigms that could begin the process of transformation. Take these few for starters.

In 2022 the UK government cut the international development budget by £4 billion, increased the defence budget by a similar amount and downgraded the Department for International development to an add-on to the Foreign and Commonwealth Office. Apart from anything else, that meant breaking a previous cross-party consensus of meeting the UN aid target of 0.7% of gross domestic product (GDP) per year. Therefore: reverse both decisions and, having done that, increase the UK aid figure to 1% of GDP per year and prioritise support for low-income states in order to surge their development of renewable energy resources. Also, reverse the cuts to the Foreign and Commonwealth Office and their impact on the diplomatic service while expanding its resources in the area in dialogue, mediation and conflict resolution.

Secondly, prioritise the UK's commitment to the UN and all its agencies and ensure that within UK government service a period working for the UN can significantly improve career prospects. Ensure that the UK's armed forces are equipped and trained to play a major role in UN peacekeeping capabilities, including the establishment of an emergency standing force, and commit a significant part of UK military forces to this work. Ensure, again, that participation in UN work is seen as an important part of a military career.

Then there is the task of developing UK military capabilities of providing emergency relief in responses to disasters, including pandemics, especially with climate breakdown leading to increasingly violent weather events. Given the RAF's, Royal Navy's and Royal Fleet Auxiliary's strengths in global logistics and the Army's experience in engineering and healthcare, these may be built into existing capabilities even while resourcing a more efficient civilian capability to project humanitarian assistance.

Finally, we should place far more emphasis on a positive UK role in arms control, not least in the areas of biological and chemical weapons. De-alert the Trident nuclear system, join the UN Nuclear Weapons Convention and proceed to a non-nuclear military posture (saving well over £200 billion over the lifetime of the Trident system).

Away from defence and foreign affairs, two potential national contributions stand out as ways to prevent climate break-down. These are in addition to enabling the Global South to make a green transition. The first is to recognise that, however soon we face up to climate breakdown, it and other examples of limits to growth will dominate global change for decades, and so a key step will be to greatly expand the UK commitment to global environmental understanding, supported by world class research. Work on climate research is centred at the Hadley Centre Climate Programme, part of the Met Office, and certain universities. Funding for that work should be doubled as a priority, and there should be increased research on oceanic and polar systems, as exemplified by the new research ship, the RRS *Sir David Attenborough*.

Hugely expand support for renewable energy research and new developments in energy storage, transport and conservation. Link this to enhancing radical decarbonisation across the whole energy system. Make the UK the lead player in this process but working closely with other states, especially ones across the Global South, with similar aims.

It may seem odd to list these aims under 'security', but all this work should be seen as conflict prevention in that it will contribute to countering the greatest current threat to global human security, the breakdown of climate systems in an already deeply divided world.

Conclusion

I might have devoted those last few pages to a 'Blueprint for a Reborn Earth', or something of the sort – eye-catching and perhaps inspiring in setting out a detailed plan for what is needed – but the reality of the kind of transformation necessary is that lots of small changes and adjustments all moving in broadly the same direction are much more likely to succeed than grand plans. Climate breakdown requires radical and rapid decarbonisation and hugely improved energy conservation, involving many individual efforts, some moving much faster than others. The process of beginning to heal the wealth divide involves many different elements – better financial regulation, immediate tax reform, combatting tax avoidance and evasion, improving labour rights – some of them capable of raising billions of pounds or dollars within months. As to security, although that requires a root and branch rethinking, there are plenty of initiatives, some listed earlier, that could get things moving.

Can it happen? Can we move to a more sustainable, equitable and peaceful world in the short space of time we have? That's the wrong question. The right question recognises that change is happening whether we like it or not, and that unless we change soon the change will be violent and uncertain as the global system comes apart. That will be very messy. Perhaps hundreds of millions of people will die and insecurity will be rife. The right question is: how quickly can we move to a more sustainable, equitable and peaceful world?

Personal experience of the insecurity trap – along with the magnifying and potentially distorting dynamic of social media – may lead to despair, apathy, conspiracy theories, blaming of others, and closed identity groups. But it is possible to take the big picture as information and knowledge that empower, providing a starting point for new understanding and action. It can also open up options for desirable shifts, including how we act in our personal lives and how we think about security.

For individuals, in communities, in movements or organisations, the best attitude is to adopt an unusual definition of prophecy as 'suggesting the possible', always looking to what can be done, whether minor or major, doing it ourselves where we can or seeking to convince others. There is much to do, but, given enough people with enough confidence, it can and will be done.

CHAPTER FIVE

What Can Be Done?

Future Possible

In the section 'Is transformation possible', Paul Rogers clearly identifies alternatives to the current insecurity trap. He recommends choices for policy and structural reform: critical innovations to address climate change, reduce inequality, reframe economics and broaden the meaning of 'security' beyond defence capability to include non-militarised responses to crisis and threat. Human security is an overarching theme. So the reader may ask, 'What can I do?'

The possibilities for reaching out and taking individual action are manifold when we consider the pace of change in the world. This section is not meant to be either definitive or daunting. Rather it is a drawing together of thoughts and possibilities for transformation, on the basis that every little step will count. No one can do it all. Overload is not the answer. The suggestions below are a sample menu of ways to be involved. They also offer links for connecting to others so that we feel more a part of the whole.

As individuals we face a daily barrage of bad news – sometimes overwhelming scenarios of gloom and suffering. One thing that can be done is to balance what you are exposed to with opportunities for talking about issues and retaining your capacity to think and act. This helps overcome the danger of feeling overwhelmed, numbed or powerless. Share your questions and concerns with others. If you want to check out and expand your sources of news, alternatives could be:

- **Solutions Journalism (https://www.solutionsjournalism.org/)** and/or those suggested by Paul, such as:
- **Open Democracy (https://www.opendemocracy.net/en/)**

Daring to reach out and act on something is a demonstration of conviction that it can be changed; agency can reflect active hope. Hopelessness and negative determinism undermine the possibility of seeds of change which can grow, influence or cascade into making a difference, however small. Rebecca Solnit argues that when you take on hope and optimism, you 'take on' their opposites and opponents: despair, defeatism, cynicism and pessimism:

> *What all these enemies of hope have in common is confidence about what is going to happen, a false certainty that excuses inaction. Whether you feel assured that everything is going to hell or will all turn out fine, you are not impelled to act. All these postures undermine participation in political life in or-dinary times, and in the climate movement in this extraordinary time. They are generally both wrong in their analysis and damaging in their consequences.*[22]

In order to bolster empowerment and participation, con-sider the many entry points close to hand. The suggestions given below are not comprehensive; they are offered as starting points for what can be done and how you can get involved. Remember that the levels of engagement are themselves fluid, for as an indi-vidual you can decide to join or participate in something much wider. A membership in **Amnesty International** or the **Cam-paign Against the Arms Trade**, for example (see page 75 and page 80) will link into international issues and needs.

Individual and neighbourhood

Climate change is a compelling issue that commands individual and collective responsibility and is a natural route to participation. From small steps – such as choosing cloth or paper rather than

---

22. https://frompoverty.oxfam.org.uk/rebecca-solnit-why-climate-despair-is-a-luxury/#comments

plastic bags, conserving water, using as many products as possible that are chemical free and safe – to initiating neighbourhood schemes for car-sharing, creating a mini-garden on a neglected piece of wasteland, or running for local office, the possibilities for participation are many. It is good to lead by example. Visible action lends itself to a multiplier effect.[23]

It is likely that inequality and food insecurity are on your doorstep, or even in your immediate experience. Volunteer in a food hub, help the food bank, explore what local faith (or other) groups are doing to offer shelter and warmth, or join a campaign. Useful starting points include:

- **https://www.trusselltrust.org/ and**
- **https://fareshare.org.uk.**

Homelessness is also increasingly widespread for reasons ranging from job insecurity to mental health issues or family crisis. For advice in the event of being made homeless see:

- **https://england.shelter.org.uk/housing_advice/homelessness** or
- **https://www.citizensadvice.org.uk/housing/homelessness/** Another useful link is:
- **https://homeless.org.uk/homeless-england/** If you work in the public sector and hold a concern about homelessness, see:
- **https://www.nhas.org.uk/news/article/how-professionals-can-help-someone-who-is-homeless**

As observed in the text, a circular economy is a system of resource production and consumption that values sharing, reusing, repairing, renewing and recycling existing materials and products as much as possible, rather than focusing on surplus or growth. Repair cafés, swap shops, upcycling and creative mending are spreading, and are things within people's practical reach.

---

23. https://www.climate-kic.org/opinion/five-ways-of-meaningfully-involving-citizens-in-climate-action/

For inspiration on ways of approaching the economy, see the **New Economics Foundation:**
- **https://neweconomics.org**

Moreover, the **Tax Justice Network** campaigns for a fairer tax system and better-funded public services:
- **https://taxjustice.net/**

Make your money work for a better world. Switch your banking and savings away from financial institutions that invest in fossil fuels, arms and harmful extractive industries. Bank instead with ethical and social banks such as **Triodos** and building societies.

Check what your pension scheme invests in. When oncologist Dr Bronwyn King found that her medical pension scheme invested in tobacco companies, she successfully campaigned for many insurance companies to divest from tobacco. **Make my Money Matter UK** researches for evidence-based advocacy for individuals, organisations and the financial sector for responsible disinvestment from areas that contribute to our climate emergency, such as fossil fuel dependence and deforestation. Their website
- **https://makemymoneymatter.co.uk/** offers sound information on various sectors, including banking and universities as well as pension schemes. These include well documented reports on current investment patterns; green banking, green pensions and proposals for reform. Their climate action paper may be found at:
- **https://makemymoneymatter.co.uk/wp-content/uploads/2024/02/Make-My-Money-Matter-Climate-Action-Report-2024.pdf**

For detail on disinvestment from the armaments industry, including which banks continue to invest in the production of cluster munitions, see:
- **https://www.ethicalconsumer.org/money-finance/banks-weapons.**

- Vote actively and discerningly on a well-informed basis.
- Run for office or serve on a civic committee.
- Listen to people.
- Keep an ear to the ground for the mood in your locality.

If it is turning ugly, if there is emergent hatred or demonising, it is possible to question and counter negative spirals. It is a matter of reaching out and convening support groups for both safety in numbers and greater influence. Do you write to the local paper, hold a peaceful demonstration in solidarity with those under attack, befriend and support the vulnerable? These are options for the individual and for outreach to community organising. Two excellent sources for resources and experience are:

- https://hopenothate.org.uk/
- https://counterhate.com/

Often the question of immigration or refugees is used as an emotive, misleading divide-and-rule tactic by groups leaning towards the far right. This was one approach used by the **Alternatives for Deutschland (AFD)** in Germany, and there are examples throughout Europe, in the UK and in the US of divisive rhetoric. If you are not already involved, find out what refugee and asylum support already exists in your locality and whether there are outreach roles for volunteers:

- https://www.refugee-action.org.uk/about/facts-about-refugees/
- https://togetherwithrefugees.org.uk/
- https://www.refugeecouncil.org.uk/

Find out about the arms trade in relation to your locality and make a statement on it – written, action-based or visual. **The Campaign against the Arms Trade** tracks arms sales and UK arms fairs, advocating and demonstrating against the selling of lethal weaponry to oppressive regimes:

- https://caat.org.uk/

Community and national

The Centre for Sustainable Energy (CSE) in the UK advises individuals and groups on energy alternatives. They help organisations of all sizes, from city councils to community groups, to transform energy systems and tackle the climate emergency. The CSE encourages the voices of young environmentalist leaders and particularly encourages 'black, brown and other minority ethnic groups to take part so that future decision-makers reflect the diversity of UK society'.

• **https://www.cse.org.uk/**

The Food Foundation aims to change food policy and business practice to ensure that everyone, across the UK nations, can afford and access a healthy and sustainable diet. They run local, school and national projects and campaigns and conduct research for advocacy and policy:

• **https://foodfoundation.org.uk/**

Two organisations supporting local food production are **Community Supported Agriculture:**

• **https://communitysupportedagriculture.org.uk/**

and the **Urban Agriculture Consortium:**

• **https://www.urbanagriculture.org.uk/community-growing/**

which covers everything from allotments to city farms.

Many issues underlie the inequality in access to housing, including high costs of ownership and insufficient rental properties. Community land trusts and cohousing arrangements offer alternative models. Community land trusts steward land for long-term wellbeing and exemplify partnerships between communities and developers, landowners, local authorities and housing associations:

• **https://www.communitylandtrusts.org.uk/**

Cohousing schemes are intentional communities run by their residents. Each household has a self-contained home as well as access to shared community space and facilities. Originating in

Denmark in the 1960s, this movement has grown across Scandinavia, Germany and the United States. The UK Cohousing Network is one example of this growing movement:

- https://cohousing.org.uk/
- https://www.communityledhomes.org.uk

The Good Law Project crowdfunds to bring legal cases for the public good – to protect the environment, hold power to account and support marginalised communities:

- https://goodlawproject.org/about/

National and international

The first UK wide coalition to focus on climate justice started as the **COP26 Coalition**, set up by **War on Want, Friends of the Earth Scotland** and the **Global Campaign to Demand Climate Justice**. Wanting longer term capacity for building a climate justice movement they transitioned to the **Climate Justice Coalition** in 2022. Their networked membership of organisations is impressive (**https://climatejustice.uk/our-members/**) and there is also a migrant worker caucus and a trade union caucus. They work with youth, with faith groups, and their outreach includes local hubs for individual and community awareness and actions:

- https://climatejustice.uk/local-hubs

Traditionally the arts and other forms of creative expression have carried messages of conscience and the need for change. These are vivid vehicles for reaching public opinion. Protest and education have been channelled through theatre, art, posters, music and song. Make your message visual, bright, bold!

- https://thegreats.co/artworks?theme=the-climate-collection

For an in-depth resource that inspires and offers practical insights, with case studies and examples of art advocacy for climate justice from the Global South see:

- https://hivos.org/document/art-advocacy-and-climate-justice/

For a clear overview of economic injustice (present and historical) and creative advocacy entry points from film to fashion, see:
• **https://economicinjustice.org.uk/**

Link into or follow an organisation working for peace, social justice and human security. **Just Security** is a forum on Law, Rights and US national security which is relevant to a wider audience:
• **https://www.justsecurity.org**

On Protest

One way in which informal messaging and campaigning on the environment, inequality or illegal arms trade gain national attention is through demonstrations and protest, which with non-violent resistance have been used throughout history to bring about needed change. Think the abolition of slavery, the suffragettes, Gandhi's Salt March, the civil rights movement, anti-apartheid protests, Black Lives Matter, and demonstrations on the environment and climate change.

From Sydney to Delhi to London, there is now a widespread trend towards clamping down on public protest. If you are engaging in this way, it is important to be aware of recent legislation so that you can prepare well.

The UK Public Order Act (POA) of 2023 was introduced in the wake of citizen protests about climate change and social justice; it explicitly named **Extinction Rebellion (XR), Just Stop Oil** and **Insulate Britain,** but also subsequent mass action in the name of **Black Lives Matter.** Just over a decade earlier, the Occupy movement protested against corporate interests in government, the global financial crisis and subprime mortgage crisis and in support of democratic renewal and the Arab Spring:
• **https://www.legislation.gov.uk/ukpga/2023/15/enacted**

The POA criminalised many forms of protest and increased police powers through new and expanded use of stop and search; orders that ban people from participating in protests and control movement, activity and associations; and the specification of new categories of offences, including 'alarm, inconvenience or annoyance to others'.

These new parameters have implications even for peaceful protest. The right to protest and to organise protests is protected by the **European Convention on Human Rights (ECHR)**. The right to freedom of expression is protected under Article 10 of the ECHR. The right to freedom of assembly is protected under Article 11. Both were brought into UK law by the 1998 Human Rights Act. This requires public authorities, like the police, to act in a way that is compatible with your rights. The police also have the legal obligation to help protests take place. A legal obligation is something that the law requires you to do. It's not optional.

For clear guidance about what to be aware of when protesting see:

- https://groups.friendsoftheearth.uk/resources/protest-guidance-know-your-rights
- https://www.libertyhumanrights.org.uk/advice_information/right-to-protest/

The Berlin based **Global Public Policy Institute (GPPI)** publishes in German and English on global governance, the political economy of conflict and international affairs:

- http://gppi.net

The **Stockholm International Peace Research Institute** offers independent resources on global security:

- https://www.sipri.org

The **European Peacebuilding Liaison Office (EPLO)** is the independent civil society platform of European NGOs, networks of NGOs and think tanks that are committed to peacebuilding and the prevention of violent conflict:

- https://eplo.org/

The **International Crisis Group (ICG)** is an independent organisation working to prevent wars and shape policies that will build a more peaceful world. They act for the prevention of violent conflict, engaging directly with a range of involved actors, in a variety of contexts:

- https://www.crisisgroup.org/who-we-are

Airwars monitors and documents the civilian casualties in war. They track, record and investigate, working for transparency and accountability from belligerent actors and advocating for affected communities:

- https://airwars.org/

Amnesty International has worked since 1961 to protect human rights; free political prisoners; campaign against injustices, including ones related to climate change and to violent conflict; and advocate for ending the unregulated flow of all weapons, from unregistered handguns in the US to combat aircraft into Yemen or Syria. There is likely to be a local chapter near you. They operate on local, national and international levels:

- https://www.amnesty.org.uk/

Amnesty International is also a member of **IANSA**, the **International Action Network on Small Arms**, a global movement against gun violence which links hundreds of civil society organisations working to stop the proliferation and misuse of small arms and light weapons around the world:

- https://iansa.org/

This is a brief introduction to what can be done by individuals, small groups and organisations to actively move away from the insecurity trap. There are viable growing points for transformation and change. Connecting with others in wider concern and movement for making a difference is something we can all do.

Judith Large

RESOURCES

Resources for working on a better way forward comes in all shapes and sizes. This section just offers some ideas. It starts with a personal selection of a few key books that provide more information about the theme of *The Insecurity Trap*. This is supplemented by a run-through of some of the groups that can provide a lot more information, and some non-mainstream media resources that can help fill some of the woeful gaps in the mainstream media.

Books and articles

ENVIRONMENT

Greta Thunberg (ed.), *The Climate Book*, New York, Penguin Allen Lane, 2022. Greta Thunberg introduces the chapters that make up this extraordinary compendium of close to a hundred short chapters by specialists from across the world on all things related to climate, the risk of climate breakdown and how to prevent it. Hugely well informed and helpfully illustrated and organised, this is a book you can dip in and out of as you want and need.

Mike Berners-Lee, *There Is No Planet B*, Cambridge, Cambridge University Press, 2019. Berners-Lee's book is much shorter than Greta Thunberg's but manages to pack in loads of information in a very readable manner that persistently suggests ways forward.

Rebecca Solnit and Thelma Young Lutunatabua, *Not Too Late: Changing the Climate Story from Despair to Possibility*, Chicago, Haymarket Books, 2023. The title sums up a really supportive book. Of all the challenges we face, the risk of climate breakdown is the one that really can overwhelm people, rather as the threat of nuclear destruction did in the 1980s. With plenty of short contributions, this book goes through the many different ways that people, as individuals or in groups, can work together effectively while getting support from the experience of others.

Matthew Lawrence and Laurie Laybourn-Langton, *Planet on Fire: A Manifesto for the Age of Environmental Breakdown*, New York,Verso, 2021. This book ably brings together environmentalism, economics and social history to re-examine root causes of the climate crisis. The authors argue passionately against extractive capitalism and for the reduction of global inequalities to enable an environmentally sustainable future. They offer viable modes of change and alternative steps we can undertake now.

Mary Robinson, *Climate Justice: A Manmade Problem with a Feminist Solution*, London, Bloomsbury, 2018. A rallying call, this book is now a classic manifesto for radical change, based on the lived experience of the marginalised and forgotten casualties of environmental change and disempowerment.

Georgina Wilson-Powell, *365 Ways to Save the Planet*, New York, DK Random House, 2023. Practical, sensible and manageable changes we can all undertaken in our personal lives and homes. Assembled in an inviting pick-and-mix format and offering steps that can be taken for positive effects for the environment.

ECONOMY

John Lanchester, *Whoops! Why Everyone Owes Everyone and No One Can Pay*, London, Allen Lane, 2010. Shortly after the financial meltdown of 2007–8, John Lanchester wrote this absolute gem of a book about what had gone wrong, why it had gone wrong and what might be done about it. What he had to say well over a decade ago remains as relevant now as then and does the best job I know of making sense of that crazy period. Four years after he wrote *Whoops!* Lanchester followed it up with *How to Speak Money: What the Money People Say and What They Really Mean*, London, Faber & Faber, 2014.

Nicholas Shaxson, *Treasure Islands: Tax Havens and the Men who Stole the World*, London, Penguin Books, 2016. A detailed but also very readable account of how the world of tax havens and related vehicles of wealth really works. Shaxson's chapter on the City of London is an absolute eye-opener.

Tom Burgis, *Kleptopia: How Dirty Money Is Conquering the World*, Glasgow, William Collins, 2021. The kind of book that makes a strong case and is supported by hundreds of footnotes and yet has a highly readable style.

Ingrid Robeyns, *Limitarianism: The Case Against Extreme Wealth*, London, Allen Lane, 2024. There are plenty of books on the impact of poverty and marginalisation, but the Dutch economist and philosopher Ingrid Robeyns looks at the other end of the spectrum, giving us an assessment of the huge dangers that stem from excessive wealth.

Maya Goepel, *Rethinking our World: An Invitation to Rescue Our Future*, London, Scribe, 2023. Translated from the German, this is a clear and readable work that explains how we are all part of the political economy and why 'business as usual' is not viable. The book includes a useful section of suggested links for further information and action.

SECURITY

Paul Rogers, *Losing Control: Global Security in the 21st Century*. This book was originally published by Pluto Press, London in 2000. The fourth edition was published in 2021 and was a substantial rewriting of the original analysis. It doesn't bring in Ukraine or Gaza but in most respects provides background and expands on the themes of The Insecurity Trap.

Andrew Feinstein, *Shadow World: Inside the Global Arms Trade*, London, Penguin Books, 2012. If we are trying to understand how military systems work, one of the best approaches is to look at the international arms trade, how it has evolved and how the arms corporations are such effective lobbyists.

William Merrin, *Digital War: A Critical Introduction*, Abingdon, Routledge, 2018. This book explores the range of uses of digital technology in contemporary warfare and conflict. It notes previous models of close military and media management (Gulf War, Kosovo and more) and examines how informational control has radically changed with the availability of new digital technologies. Useful for understanding how technological developments such as unmanned drones and cyberwar have impacted upon global conflict. Also good as an introduction to emerging technologies such as soldier systems, robotics and artificial intelligence and their possible future impact.

Cynthia Enloe, *Globalisation and Militarism: Feminists Make the Link*, 2nd edition, London, Rowman & Littlefield, 2016. This is a now classic interrogation of the gender dynamics at work in the processes of global militarisation.

Amitav Acharya, 'Human Security', in *The Globalisation of World Politics: An Introduction to International Relations*, edited by John Baylis, Steve Smith and Patrician Owens, Oxford, Oxford University Press, 2020, https://www.researchgate.net/publication/339956544_Human_Security

Ammerdown Group, 'Rethinking Security: A Discussion Paper', 2016, https://www.researchgate.net/publication/318129168_Rethinking_security_A_discussion_paper. This 70+ page paper takes a close look at what we mean by 'security'.

POLITICAL TRENDS AND COMBATING MISINFORMATION AND DISINFORMATION

Steven Levitsky and Daniel Ziblatt, *How Democracies Die: What History Reveals about our Future*, New York, Crown, 2018. Levitsky and Ziblatt draw on historical precedents to gain a perspective on US democratic decline, pointing to the danger signs inherent in the erosion of norms. Norms are the unspoken rules and conventions that hold democracies together, in public and institutional behaviour. Their erosion creates the kind of vacuum that abuse of power may enter.

David Renton, *The New Authoritarians: Convergence on the Right*, London, Pluto Press 2019. Renton is a master of analysis, tracking changes in how 'The right has changed; it has embraced the ideas of its outliers' in Europe and the US. He documents shifting political alliances and the dangerous centrality of racism as a core element in new forms of the far right.

Timothy Snyder, *On Tyranny: Twenty Lessons from the Twentieth Century*, New York, Penguin Books, Random House, 2017. Written as a clarion call to action on the eve of the Trump presidency, this book draws on lessons from European history and reminds us that no society is free from possible descent into tyranny: twenty lessons for our times.

Lee McIntyre, *On Disinformation: How to Fight for Truth and Protect Democracy*, Boston, Massachusetts Institute of Technology 2023. There is transatlantic relevance in this small handbook about how to stop the 'algorithmic spread of propaganda on social media', given the opaque high-tech engineering involved.

Elaine Kasket, *Reboot: Reclaiming Your Life in a Tech-Obsessed World*, London, Elliott & Thompson, 2023. This is a thoughtful study of digital social media experience within a human development framework. It examines technology's effects at different stages of life from infancy onwards and suggests ways to be in control of it rather than being controlled by it.

Vidhya Ramalingam (https://www.isdglobal.org): 'On the Front Line: A Guide to Countering Far-Right Extremism', Institute for Strategic Dialogue, 2014, https://www.isdglobal.org/wp-content/

uploads/2016/03/On_The_Front_Line_Far_RightHANDBOOK.
pdf. This valuable resource remains relevant and useful.

Hein de Haas, *How Migration Really Works: A Factful Guide to the Most Divisive Issue in Politics*, London, Viking, 2023. For clarity on terminology, history and the myths about migration, this useful and comprehensive book is invaluable. Especially useful in discussion to counter disinformation and misinformation.

Links

Rethinking Security is a group of practitioners, campaigners and academics working on new security thinking for the UK and responsible for the *Alternative Security Review* for the UK. http://www.rethinkingsecurity.org.uk/

Saferworld is an independent organisation working in Africa, Asia and the Middle East with local national partners, and at policy levels of the European Union and UN. They are committed to working to prevent and transform violent conflict, advocate for peace and justice and build safer lives. https://www.saferworld-global.org/

Conciliation Resources works in many areas of conflict across the world and is committed to stopping violent conflict and creating more peaceful societies. http://www.c-r.org/

Carbon Brief covers climate science, energy and policy, specialising in clear, data-driven articles to improve understanding of climate change. Its Friday news summary is particularly useful. http://www.carbonbrief.org/

International Alert is a global peacebuilding charity. Established in 1986, it aims to promote dialogue, training, research, policy analysis, advocacy and outreach. https://www.international-alert.org/

Declassified UK is a group of investigative journalists specialising in UK security policy who have a reputation for uncovering the hidden implications of national security practice. http://www.declassifieduk.org/

Peace Direct is an international charity dedicated to supporting local peacebuilders across the world. https://www.peacedirect.org/about-us/

Byline Times offers a news source for alternative views and opinions omitted by the mainstream. https://bylinetimes.com/

Open Democracy is an independent international media platform with high-quality contributions that challenge power, inspire change and offers a platform to groups underrepresented in the national media. https://www.opendemocracy.net/en/

Campaign Against the Arms Trade is a UK organisation working to end the international arms trade. They point out that export drives are led purely by the ability to pay, without scrutiny of intended use or repercussions. https://caat.org.uk/

The Institute for Strategic Dialogue (ISD) is an independent, non-profit organisation dedicated to safeguarding human rights and reversing the tide of polarisation, extremism and disinformation worldwide. https://www.isdglobal.org/

Other writing by Paul Rogers

On the Israeli way of war, and why it isn't working in Gaza: *The Guardian Comment is Free*, 28 May 2024. https://www.theguardian.com/commentisfree/article/2024/may/28/attacks-rafah-no-accident-idf-losing-strategy.

'Israel has rewritten the rules of war – but is no closer to destroying Hamas', *Open Democracy* 5 April 2024. https://www.opendemocracy.net/en/israel-gaza-war-palestine-netanyahu-cant-destroy-hamas-biden-ceasefire/

'Will Israel respond to US pressure to tread carefully in Rafah? There is a precedent', *The Conversation*, 22 February 2024. https://theconversation.com/gaza-war-will-israel-respond-to-us-pressure-to-tread-carefully-in-rafah-there-is-a-precedent-224171

'Is there any hope of a ceasefire in Gaza?', *Open Democracy* 17 November 2023. https://www.opendemocracy.net/en/israel-gaza-is-a-ceasefire-possible-palestine-hamas-netanyahu-biden/

'The Israel Hamas war again shows we need to stop thinking that there are military solutions to political problems', *The Guardian Comment is Free*, 8 November 2023. https://www.theguardian.com/commentisfree/2023/nov/08/israel-hamas-war-palestine-military-solutions-political-problems?fbclid=IwAR0LqU2Dy4pOmz401sLnGDDv9vtaep0-KXoW_Ykq36ttIEqrvIg5hry3bq8

'West's response to Kakhovska Dam destruction highlights anxieties on Ukraine', *Open Democracy*, 9 June 2023. https://www.opendemocracy.net/en/kakhovska-dam-breach-russia-west-unease-ukraine-far-right/

'Could Putin's war crimes charges give ICC more authority over Western leaders?', *Open Democracy*, 25 March, 2023. https://www.opendemocracy.net/en/international-criminal-court-putin -war-crimes-ukraine-iraq-wars-media-coverage/

'Iranian nuclear deal threatened by political turmoil in Iran and Israel', *Open Democracy*, 13 March 2023 – https://www.opendemocracy.net/en/iran-nuclear-enrichment-jcpoa-israel/

'A Thirty-year War' (Iraq), *Open Democracy*, 3 April 2003. https://www.opendemocracy.net/en/article_1127jsp/

'Ukraine and Global Human Security', for *Rethinking Security*, 31 May 2022. https://rethinkingsecurity.org.uk/2022/05/31/ukraine-and-global-human-security/

'No End in Sight' (Afghanistan), *Open Democracy*, 20 March 2002.https://www.opendemocracy.net/en/article_118jsp/

Note: Paul Rogers was interviewed online by Owen Jones of *The Guardian* on 18 December, 2023 on 'Why Israel can't Win'. The broadcast received 676,000 views and 20,000 'likes': https://www.youtube.com/watch?v=ML1Vc3B-y2w

AUTHOR BIOGRAPHIES

Paul Rogers is Professor Emeritus of Peace Studies at Bradford University, working there for over forty years. He trained initially in the Life Sciences at Imperial College before working in crop research in East Africa and then lectured on environmental security. He has worked on the causes of war, especially how they relate to global limits to growth, a failing economic system and military cultures often dominated by the need for control. He's lectured at Britain's senior defence colleges for forty years, engaged with government ministries, given evidence to parliamentary committees and is a past chair of the British International Studies Association.

Judith Large is a Senior Fellow at the Conflict Analysis Research Centre (CARC) University of Kent in Canterbury, UK, with three decades of experience in conflict zones and post-war recovery settings. She worked with affected communities, NGOs, national governments, and UN agencies for peacebuilding, inclusive political settlement, and participative development. She held senior positions at International IDEA in Stockholm, the Conflict Management Initiative (Brussels), and was an advisor to the Berghof Foundation (Berlin). Judith assisted with specific international conflict mediation and negotiation processes.

ACKNOWLEDGEMENTS

I would like to thank Judith Large for our early discussions about the idea of a short book, for continuing support and thoughts as the idea progressed, and also for contributing the *Foreword* and the final section *What Can be Done?*. I would further like to thank Martin Large of Hawthorn Press for being willing to take on the process of turning it into a book, with much help and good advice along the way.

The theme of three interacting global challenges in the post-Cold War years – economy, environment and security – has its origins in work with Malcolm Dando (*A Violent Peace*, 1992), and with Geoff and Kath Tansey (*A World Divided*, 1994). Work with the Oxford Research Group and especially Scilla Elworthy in the post-9/11 environment was notable, as have been many discussions with Jenny Pearce at Bradford.

More generally I have benefitted hugely from a 45-year connection with the Peace Studies group at Bradford University and the many students from across the world. Staff and students there have persistently shown a commitment to issues of peace and development that I have not met in any other institution, and it has been a privilege to be involved.

Paul Rogers, April 2024

PASS THIS BOOK ON!

Ordering The Insecurity Trap

The Insecurity Trap will be formally published on 23rd September 2024 and available from bookshops. It will also be available as an ebook from 23rd September, for easy dissemination worldwide.

However, you are invited to pass this book on!
Please also consider ordering copies to give or share with friends, members of your party, faith group, book group, students or public meetings and above all to advocate for key policies and action points with your MP and/or parliamentary candidates.

Discounts and ordering

Books can be ordered from our website **www.hawthornpress.com** or direct with our distributor Booksource: Phone 00 44 141 642 9192 or Email: info@booksource.net

20% discount when ordering 3 copies or more sent to the same address.

Hawthorn Press

OTHER BOOKS FROM HAWTHORN PRESS

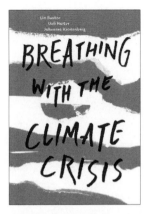

Breathing with the Climate Crisis
Lin Bautze, Ueli Hurter, Johannes Kronenberg

Breathing with the Climate Crisis offers a hopeful narrative about the climate crisis, a new, different perspective that could unleash the courage to act.
64pp; 168 x 118mm; pb 978-1-912480-87-6

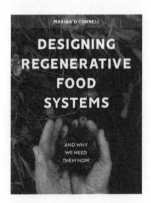

Designing Regenerative Food Systems
Marina O'Connell

This is a toolkit for designing regenerative food systems. It outlines biodynamic, organic, permaculture, agroforestry, agroecology and regenerative farming methods. The principles and practices of each approach are explained concisely for farmers, growers and students.
224pp; 246 x 189mm; pb 978-1-912480-54-8; ebk: 978-1-912480-98-2

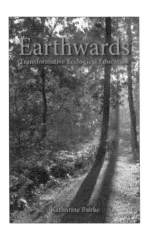

Earthwards
Transformative Ecological Education
Katharine Burke

Earthwards shows teachers how they can help students develop their ecological literacy and personal resilience. It shares transformative stories, concepts and methods of connecting with nature for life.
208pp; 234 x 156mm; pb 978-1-912480-91-3; ebk 978-1-912480-98-2

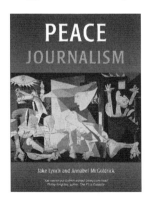

Peace Journalism
Annabel McGoldrick, Jake Lynch

Jake Lynch and Annabel McGoldrick are experienced international news journalists. *Peace Journalism* explains how most coverage of conflict unwittingly fuels further violence and proposes workable options to give peace a chance.
264pp; 246 x 189mm; ebk 978-1-907359-47-7

Small Steps to Less Waste
Stories to Inspire Change
Claudi Williams

This book offers simple alternatives to mass-produced, shop-bought, highly packaged goods. It includes positive projects to help you to take back control of your waste and reduce people's impact on the environment.
96pp; 256 x 186mm; pb 978-1-912480-29-6

ORDERING BOOKS

If you have difficulties ordering Hawthorn Press books from a bookshop, you can order direct from our website: **www.hawthornpress.com**

or from our UK distributor:

BookSource: 50 Cambuslang Road, Glasgow, G32 8NB

Tel: (0845) 370 0063, Email: orders@booksource.net

Details of our overseas distributors can be found on our website.

Hawthorn Press
www.hawthornpress.com